Landlord~Tenant Solutions

IN CALIFORNIA

BY STEVEN ADAIR MACDONALD

INVESTMENT
PUBLISHING HOUSE
NEW YORK • SAN FRANCISCO

This publication is designed to provide accurate information in regard to the subject matter covered. However, readers should consult an attorney for their individual needs in relation to legal matters.

The author and publisher gratefully acknowledge Dwarf Music for permission to reprint the lyrics to "Dear Landlord" by Bob Dylan: Copyright ©1968 by DWARF MUSIC. All rights reserved. International copyright secured. Reprinted by permission.

Printed and bound in the United State of America.
00 99 98   10 9 8 7 6 5 4 3 2 1

Publisher's Cataloging in Publication Data

MacDonald, Steven Adair, 1948 -
    Landlord-tenant solutions in California / Steven Adair
MacDonald. — 1st ed.
        p. cm.
        Includes index.
        Library of Congress Catalog Number: 96-78154
        ISBN 0-9654726-6-3
        First Printing: June 1998

        1. Landlord and tenant—California —Popular works. 2. Leases—
California—Popular works. I. Title.

KFC145.Z9M33 1997   346.79404'34
                    QBI97-511

Book and cover design by LeeAnn Nelson
Author's photo by Anthony Abuzeide

To order more copies of this book:
Contact Investment Publishing House, Opera Plaza, 601 Van Ness Avenue, #E3610, San Francisco, CA 94102.

～

This book is dedicated to my children,
Angus Michihiro MacDonald, David Shin'ichi MacDonald,
and Heather Mineko MacDonald,
whose accomplishments in life will no doubt
be far greater than my own.

～

ACKNOWLEDGMENTS

This book could not have been written without the support of numerous special people in my life: teachers, colleagues, co-workers, and friends. Although the result is a humble one, I would like to express heartfelt appreciation to some of those who contributed to its success.

I am grateful to the first teachers who encouraged me to pursue a legal career: David B. Green, Jeffrey Klurfeld (presently Regional Director, Federal Trade Commission), and Professors J. Lani Bader and Myron Moskovitz of Golden Gate University School of Law.

Many colleagues—especially my professional adversaries—stimulated my study of landlord-tenant law: Jethro Busch, Robert DeVries, Arnold Ellis, Carolyn Gold, Marc Janowitz, J. Wallace Oman, Ora Prochovnick, and Randall M. Shaw. I have the greatest respect for them and for all who practice their profession with a strong sense of justice.

I happily offer thanks to my coworkers, past and present, who have made daily life so enjoyable: Richard Beckman, Leanne Do, Virender Goswami, Sarah Jones, Mayvelyn Marton, KyungAe Pahk, Joseph Sacramento, and Mei Chi Yee.

Finally, I wish to thank the friends who stand with me as mentors and comrades struggling to create a peaceful world: Daisaku Ikeda, Bob Corkish, Ed Horan, Kim Jordan, Kumiko MacDonald, Danny Nagashima, Luis Nieves, and so many more.

To all of you, as well as those who are not mentioned by name, I thank you for making it possible for me to bring to fruition the thoughts embodied in this book.

Steven Adair MacDonald
San Francisco, California
May 3, 1998

CONTENTS

PREFACE

My involvement in the practice of housing law has been quite provocative. I have come to see that almost everyone is affected by landlord-tenant relationships at some time or another, whether as a landlord, a tenant, or a dependent of one of these. Having been involved as an advocate of the various parties to related disputes on thousands of occasions, and as a pro tem Municipal Court judge, I have drawn some distinct conclusions which I believe can benefit the general public. These experiences have led me to write a series of articles on the subject of landlord-tenant law which have been published in local newspapers and magazines in California over the last several years. The articles have now been transformed into this book in the hope of sharing my experience with a wider audience.

If a landlord or tenant has to seek legal representation, the situation is bound to become expensive. Therefore, this book emphasizes ways to either avoid problems before they occur or to resolve them at an early stage. The use of practical approaches based on genuine respect for the other person(s) involved is strongly stressed as the best way to minimize or avoid legal disputes.

INTRODUCTION

"In every civilized society property rights must be carefully safeguarded; ordinarily and in the great majority of cases, human rights and property rights are fundamentally and in the long run, identical; but when it clearly appears that there is a real conflict between them, human rights must have the upper hand; for property belongs to man and not man to property."

Theodore Roosevelt
Speech at the University of Paris
April 23, 1910

Many people in America have discovered the pleasures and rewards of moving toward their financial goals by purchasing and managing income property. Entrepreneurial consultants list rental real estate as one of the ten best investments you can make. Financial planners show that ninety percent of financially independent people have become so through real estate. Whether or not you are already financially secure or determined to become so, chances are that if you are reading this book, you have discovered the benefits of rental property as a means to achieve financial success. The last thing you want is to have your investment threatened by destructive tenants or troublesome rental situations. To overcome such threats as you may be facing now, or to prevent them before they occur, many rental property owners turn to self-help legal books such as this one.

The market in self-help legal books is filled with advice for people on one side or the other of a broad range of disputes, showing them how to gain the advantage over their adversaries. The section of the market dealing with landlord-tenant issues is no exception. Like other books addressing rental property issues, *Landlord~Tenant Solutions in California* speaks to readers who are grappling with issues from the landlord's or rental property owner's perspective. This book provides sound recommendations about how to handle some of the most troubling and the most common problems that a rental property owner can face: disruptive and destructive tenants, lease violations, nonpayment of rent, courtroom scenarios, and more. This book, however, is different from most of its kind in several important ways:

First, I am the only author of such a book who actually litigates in the courtroom trenches of San Francisco and throughout California, and who takes over situations when they have become severe. I handle these difficult cases in one of three possible ways.

▪ *by going to trial,*

▪ *by dealing with technical challenges in court in which one side or the other is dismissed, or*

▪ *by reaching a court-approved settlement resolving all disputes between the parties.*

Second, unlike many landlord and tenant manuals, this book is not intended to be a comprehensive how-to guide for landlords. Rather, it is a companion, a reader, for owners who are trying to avoid typical problems discussed here.

The third and most unique virtue of this book is that it demonstrates attitudes of understanding and compassion for tenants, and it suggests peaceful resolutions whenever possible. My commitment is to share with you the concrete personal, legal, and financial benefits of finding solutions to your problems based on a foundation of respect for the tenants with whom you may be struggling. This book captures the essential spirit of how I counsel owners who come to my office when situations have become severe while saving them many thousands of dollars through a creative and fair approach.

However, it is often difficult to show respect when faced with a threat to something as important to you as your rental property investment. It is natural to respond with anger and defensiveness, viewing the other person in a hostile manner. In the heat of conflict, he or she may appear to be intentionally out to harm you, and you may find yourself wanting to react aggressively to protect yourself. While all these reactions are understandable, acting on them is not in your best interest. There are better ways to handle such situations, including learning to prevent them from occurring in the first place.

Take, for example, a situation in which new tenants agree to a handsome monthly rental amount, move into a recently vacated unit on very short notice, and then are repeatedly behind in paying their rent. You may feel that the tenants are intentionally cheating you and thus may want to react by evicting them as quickly as possible, to avoid losing any more time or money. As a result of what feels like their hostile act of withholding rent, you may wish to respond in kind by threatening to eject them to save the time and expense of a judicial process. Although this may seem like the quickest way to protect your investment, it is actually dangerous and potentially harmful:

- *On the personal level, the emotional distress which is produced from reacting out of anger as well as the danger of inciting tenants to physical aggression can be dangerous to one's health.*

- *On the legal level, "self-help" actions— i.e., the shortcuts taken by landlords to evict tenants—are strictly illegal in California. They can subject the income property owner to huge damage awards and negative publicity.*

- *On the financial level, since insurance companies are not legally able to defend intentional wrongful acts, you may find yourself unprotected from tremendous monetary losses. Thus, you may have to pay the judgment yourself or have your property sold to satisfy it.*

How else might one handle this situation? For one thing, a thorough screening of tenants, as pointed out in Chapter 1, might prevent the situation altogether. The proper legal remedies are described throughout the book, particularly in Chapters 17, 22–24, and 30.

In this book, I give sound legal guidance and suggestions for a peaceful, respectful, and compassionate approach that I have found results in the greatest success for both the short term and the long run. However, since landlord-tenant litigation is a very fluid area of the law, make sure you consult with an attorney before pursuing any legal action.

Looking at things from a historical perspective, taking a person to court is a civilized society's way of beating him or her up. The judicial process is time-consuming, costly, and frequently filled with great distress. What most Americans do not see, though, is that the American legal system is actually based on a commitment to resolving disputes in the most peaceful way possible. It is from this cornerstone of sound American law that I have written my book. The wisdom in this approach has been borne out during my many years of providing legal counsel to both landlords and tenants, as well as by my experience as a *pro tem* Municipal Court judge. Whether you are working toward managing your property to avoid problems, or are addressing problems which periodically arise, the best way to succeed is to understand your tenants and treat them with compassion and respect.

Fighting is often the first position you may feel yourself thrust into when someone treats you with disrespect and a lack of consideration. But in the long run, fighting can be painful and is often unnecessary. As Mohandas Gandhi once said: "Victory attained by violence is tantamount to a defeat, for it is momentary." For example, an unlawful eviction may get rid of the problem for the moment, but it will undoubtedly come back to haunt you, often through a costly and unsuccessful lawsuit. Conversely, you will feel more peaceful and less stressed if you try to see the issues from the other person's point of view while taking the legal steps necessary to protect your investment.

I have long had a commitment to working toward peace in a world where the human condition for many people is one of constant struggle. It would be easy for a lawyer to encourage his clients to view the other side as the enemy; forces in the world push us daily to adopt the dualistic "us versus them" stance that permeates our society. I hope that this book will serve as a breath of fresh air that will help readers to see their way clearly to a peaceful solution and to educate themselves about the legal and financial advantages that result from working in a respectful manner.

I firmly believe that a knowledgeable, firm, and courteous approach is the wisest. On the practical side, maintaining good relations with your tenants will keep you, the owner, out of costly legal disputes. Even if doing so sometimes means bending over backwards, it is your best protection against having tenants damage your property or leave without giving notice, and therefore owing you money. Most people respond more positively to respect and compassion than to animosity or threats. In brief, this book covers the best approaches to managing rental property. You can use it by reading it as a whole piece to get an overview of methods for handling the toughest problems you will encounter. Or, you can use it like a smorgasbord, picking out whichever chapters you need to handle specific problems. Either way, you will end up a lot happier and with fewer costs and hassles in your rental property investment. If you need to get legal help, you will be prepared to discern the most effective strategy to adopt.

—S.A.M.

A Good Start

"*Prevent trouble before it arises.*"

—Tao Te Ching

1

Good Tenants

F ROM A LANDLORD'S PERSPECTIVE, one of the most important steps in the owner-tenant relationship is the selection of an appropriate tenant. Marketing an available unit is important to attract qualified, reliable applicants. Setting an acceptable rent amount is also important, but it should be done with an eye to obtaining the best tenant for the long run. After a tenant is selected, a lease or rental agreement provides numerous opportunities to protect the owner's interest. The purpose of this chapter is to advise both how to select a qualified tenant and how to avoid potential legal problems.

Once an appropriate amount of rent and other basic issues have been decided, a tenant must be selected. The first problem for the owner to avoid in this process is an accusation of discrimination. All tenant applicants must be treated as equally as possible. The owner has a right to make character judgments, but they cannot be based on an applicant's race, age, gender, or religion, or on the presence (or absence) of children. All such issues and exclusions must be avoided in advertisements and discussions of the unit.

Word-of-mouth may be the best form of advertising—it is certainly the cheapest. However, if mass media are used, they should be used selectively. Certain specialty-type publications tend to attract certain types of prospects. Another key legal rule in advertising is honesty: Promises should not be made unless you can keep them, and descriptions of the unit should be accurate.

In most of California the rent which may be charged is limited only by market forces. Even rent control ordinances do not always affect what can be charged a new tenant. Only Berkeley and a few other cities have adopted what is known as "vacancy control" [see Section 2], and recent state law now mandates a phasing-out of these local restrictions. San Francisco has considered, but rejected, "vacancy control" several times. Both landlords and potential tenants should verify a property's status in regard to possible rent limitations.

Assuming a vacant unit is presently exempt from a rent ceiling, some owners will rent for slightly less than the market rate in order to pick the best tenant among several qualified applicants. Once a tenant has been selected, the amount of rent and the due date should be put down in writing, specifying that it is due in advance. (Form rental agreements typically cover these and other basic terms.) Grace periods are not required; however, late charges should be reasonable—for example, 2 to 3 percent of the rent amount. It is also customary to specify where the rent is to be sent.

Although the specific clauses of a rental agreement are important, the tenants' application—particularly their personal information—may be even more significant. Each prospective tenant, including all proposed adult co-occupants, should submit a rental application. This application should include a social security number, employment information, bank accounts, and personal references. Previous landlords and current employers are the usual references and may be consulted for confirmation. Using this information, a landlord can best determine which applicants will be responsible tenants. And in the event that any disputes arise in the future, the landlord may have some chance of recovering losses. Most important, when screening potential tenants, the landlord should not be in a hurry. Sufficient time should be taken to screen the applicants and verify all of the information provided.

I know of many cases in which a landlord has gratefully accepted the rental application of people who were willing to pay the asking price for an apartment. They were able to pay thousands of dollars in cash for the first and last months' rent and the security deposit. However, in many cases, this was the last money the owner received from tenants whose references were not checked and who turned out to be totally irresponsible. Accepting someone who is willing to pay a high rent but is in a hurry to move in and pays cash, may be enticing because perhaps no one else will pay as much. This temptation may even seem to justify foregoing a credit evaluation. Credit reports, however, are essential research tools. They are vital sources of information which will help ensure the selection of a valued tenant. (The tenant may be charged for the credit report.)

The selection of a tenant from among a group of applicants should be based solely on their employment and credit history as well as professional and personal references. A property owner should keep records of all who apply so that if a rejected minority group member alleges discrimination, there will be evidence that the decision was fair and impartial.

An owner is advised to get the first and last months' rent and/or security deposit in the form of a cashier's check. Before signing a lease or rental agreement, a thorough inspection of the rental unit should be conducted with the tenant. Both parties should initial a checklist and attach it to the lease. This will help avoid disputes later about the physical condition of the unit at the time the tenant took possession. Some landlords use a Polaroid camera or camcorder for this purpose. Such evidence is very persuasive.

An owner who succeeds in attracting a qualified and responsible tenant willing to pay the fair value for a rental unit will have done as much as is possible to avoid problems later in the tenancy. Successful marketing and intelligent pricing—the initial steps—provide an opportunity for selecting an excellent tenant. Negotiating the details of the rental agreement, while also important, will probably be the easy part.

2 Key Terms in a Lease

ONCE A TENANT HAS BEEN SELECTED, one of the first questions confronting a landlord is whether the rental agreement should be oral or written. The problem with a verbal agreement is that the terms can easily be disputed. Accordingly, there is no logical reason not to have the rental agreement in writing. Appropriate forms are available from stationery stores and are basically sound [see Appendix B], although attention should be given to certain key areas.

A good lease or rental agreement will include all the elements necessary to protect the landlord's interests. An accurate description of the premises should be given. The length of the rental term, whether it is by year or a month-to-month tenancy, is an essential element and must be specified. (Note that in rent-controlled jurisdictions even a month-to-month tenancy may allow the tenants to remain for many years.) Obviously, a rental agreement also includes the amount of rent, and it should show any additional charges, such as utilities or garage rent.

Is the rent due on the first of the month or some other date? This should be expressed. The number of people who will occupy the unit should be shown. While a reasonable restriction against overcrowding may be included, landlords should be careful not to discriminate against children. Typically, a restriction or a prohibition against subleasing or assignment of the lease to another person is a good idea. Some landlords prohibit pets; if pets are allowed, an extra security deposit should be requested to cover potential damages caused by the pet(s). Other permitted clauses might prohibit repairs or alterations by the tenant without the landlord's prior written consent.

The names of all adult occupants should be included, and all of them should sign the agreement. A reasonable charge of 5 percent for late payment of rent would probably be upheld by the courts, but more than that is doubtful. Some landlords make "house rules" part of the lease by mentioning them in the body of the rental agreement and then attaching a set to the contract. These rules are useful because they clarify such things as the garage space, if any, that the tenant may use, whether a backyard or other common area is available, and possible restrictions on their use. Another typical house rule concerns "quiet hours": for example, no loud music can be played after 10:00 P.M. on weekdays.

Other things to note:

■ *Is the deposit for security or for the last month's rent? Because it can affect the landlord's legal position, this should be made very clear.*

■ *A statement that each adult tenant or cotenant is jointly and individually liable to perform the contract is very important.*

■ *A checklist, to be signed by the tenant, is a useful way to avoid future problems. The tenant should inspect everything in the apartment and sign the checklist accordingly.*

There are some things that a landlord should probably not have in a lease: An attorney's fee clause does not usually benefit the landlord and is more likely to benefit the tenant. If the landlord attempts legal action to enforce the lease and is awarded attorney's fees, the money may be difficult to collect. However, if for some reason the tenant is awarded attorney's fees, he or she will know where to collect. For this reason, some landlords omit the clause from the lease.

Landlords should also avoid allowing a tenant to share utilities with another set of tenants. If the rental unit is an in-law apartment, the property owner might consider negotiating a higher rent that would include the cost of utilities. Otherwise, a dispute between tenants could arise that would be blamed on the landlord.

It is not advisable for a landlord to allow tenants to make repairs for credit on the rent. Doing so may be illegal and often gives rise to disputes. No lease or rental agreement should require a tenant to waive any rent control protections or any state laws regarding tenants' rights: Doing so is illegal and makes a landlord subject to penalty. Finally, in writing a rental agreement, note that all security deposits are refundable: A nonrefundable deposit is illegal. Cleaning fees and all other types of fees or deposits are considered part of the security deposit and are refundable. [Security deposits are discussed more thoroughly in Chapter 3.]

For landlords, a most difficult situation is when a tenant changes locks without providing the landlord with duplicates of the new keys. To avoid this situation, include a provision in your lease or rental agreement stipulating either that locks may not be changed or that you are to be provided with duplicate keys if locks are changed. If this situation occurs in a month-to-month tenancy and such a provision is not already in the lease, you can serve your tenants with a Thirty Day Notice that the provision is being added.

In sum, the rental agreement should be in writing to avoid misunderstandings. Indeed, if the rent term is for more than one year, the law requires the lease to be in writing. This effort will best protect both landlord and tenant interests.

3

Security Deposits

THIS CHAPTER WILL DISCUSS several important concepts concerning security deposits, including how security deposits are defined, what amounts can be requested, and when they are refundable.

As defined by California law, security deposits include *everything* that a tenant pays at the beginning of the tenancy except the first month's rent. Thus, a cleaning fee, pet deposit, key deposit, *last month's rent*, and any so-called administrative charges are all defined by law as security deposits. All deposits are refundable, even if the rental agreement says otherwise. Under state or local law, most tenancy rights, including those governing security deposits, cannot be waived or released by a tenant. (These limitations do not apply, however, to commercial leases.)

The amount of a security deposit may vary considerably from unit to unit, but there are definite legal restrictions that govern these amounts. The security deposit for an unfurnished unit cannot exceed the amount of two months' rent. For a furnished apartment, the maximum allowable deposit is the equivalent of three months' rent. Note: these amounts do not include the first month's rent payment.

At the beginning of the tenancy the landlord and the tenant should walk together through the entire premises with a checklist, noting the condition of every aspect of the premises. Photographs are also useful. These efforts will help prevent later disputes about damages to the apartment and possible deductions from the deposit when the tenant vacates.

No state law specifies exactly how a landlord should hold deposits, although local ordinances sometimes require them to be held in a separate bank account. San Francisco requires landlords to pay an annual 5 percent interest on security deposits to their tenants. Under local ordinances, increasing a deposit, even to an amount less than the maximum under state law, can be a problem. It may be considered an indirect or illegal rent increase.

If a rented building is sold, the owner must account to the tenants or to the buyers for all deposits. Typically, a report of all security deposit amounts is provided by the seller, and the total amount is credited to the buyer as part of the purchase price. Then the new owner holds the deposits and is responsible for them.

As disputes over security deposits usually arise at the end of a tenancy, a joint inspection, photographs, and a witness can help establish the conditions of various aspects of the rental unit when the tenants are vacating. Deductions to the security deposit are limited by law to three circumstances: unpaid rent, repair costs for damages beyond normal wear and tear, and cleaning. A refund and/or itemization of deductions must be sent to the tenant within 21 days of the move-out date. It is important to get receipts for any expenses. If the work is done by the owner or a member of his family, a reasonable hourly rate should be charged. Sometimes damages should be prorated, based on how long the tenant has occupied the premises. For example, if a new carpet was provided, and is now ruined, the life expectancy of that rug (10 years?) must be determined and compared to the length of the tenant's occupancy. If there are delays obtaining the cost of repairs, the landlord should write to the former tenant within 21 days of his or her vacating the premises, giving an estimate of the expected costs or explaining the circumstances. If the tenant's address is unknown, the landlord can address the letter to the vacated premises and the Post Office will forward it, if possible.

For landlords, the failure to properly refund a security deposit can have serious consequences. If a tenant can prove that part or all of her deposit was not refunded, or that certain deductions were unfairly claimed by the landlord, she can obtain an award in Small Claims Court of up to $600 in punitive damages—in addition to the complete refund of and interest on the security deposit itself.

The simplest way to avoid that problem is to keep accurate records of the condition of the rental unit, both before and after the tenant's occupancy, and to send out an accurate itemization of deductions within 21 days. If a dispute arises, this evidence can be shown to the tenant in an effort to avoid a lawsuit. Being fair and willing to compromise are probably the most effective ways to stay out of Small Claims Court.

4

Sufficient Insurance

AN UNINSURED LANDLORD can suffer financial ruin as a result of a lawsuit by a tenant or tenant's guest. In addition to personal injury cases, landlords in California are often accused of harassment, retaliation, and wrongful eviction, particularly in rent-controlled jurisdictions. These actions include claims for emotional distress, punitive damages, court costs, and the plaintiff's attorney's fees. Legal fees alone to defend a suit are sometimes as much or greater than the amount of the claim. The solution to this potential problem is to have adequate insurance.

The first step for an income property owner is to contact a knowledgeable and reputable insurance agent. If necessary, get a referral from a real estate broker, a lawyer, or a friend who also owns property. Specify, in writing, that you want coverage for potential claims of emotional distress, wrongful eviction, etc. that might be presented by your tenants. A typical policy designed for landlords should cover all unintentional acts of the owner and the owner's agents, and employees—even if an act turns out to be illegal. Normally, coverage also includes the standard fire and comprehensive liability required by the mortgage holder (if there is one). Some insurance companies market a policy designed especially to meet the needs of California landlords. Many companies do not. If your policy does not cover these special risks, have it amended to include them. If this is not possible, change your insurance carrier to one that provides the necessary coverage or find another broker. [See Appendix C].

Having adequate insurance is of vital importance for rental property owners for a number of reasons. If a judge or jury determines that the landlord has intentionally harassed, discriminated against, or wrongfully evicted a tenant, the landlord can be held personally liable for a penalty in excess of the tenant's actual loss. These are punitive damages, meant to punish the intentional wrong. In addition, the losing party usually has to pay both his own and the other side's attorneys' fees as well as all court costs. The same damages can be assessed for behavior the court finds to have been reckless, even if it was not entirely intentional. An insurance company cannot and will not pay for intentional wrongs. (Such awards are common in rent-controlled cities such as San

Francisco where the local ordinance requires the court to triple the actual damages.)

I know of many cases where the attorney's fees on each side represented several *years'* worth of rent. In cases in which a landlord's attorney made even a small, technical error, the lawsuits were dismissed by the court. The landlord was subsequently sued for the tenant's emotional distress and all his legal fees.

To avoid getting sued when resolving a dispute with a tenant, a landlord can obtain a "release" or a "mutual release." Many attorneys recommend, for example, waiving back rent when evicting a tenant in exchange for the tenant's release of any claims he or she may have against the landlord, frivolous or otherwise. This agreement is enforceable and bars future suits, thereby avoiding unpleasant surprises later.

Litigation is not pleasant. False accusations, expenses, tedious depositions, the threat of punitive damages—they can all easily result in loss of income and the deterioration of one's health. However, litigation is sometimes unavoidable. The wise landlord's best defense is insurance coverage that protects him or her from the potential financial ruin that virtually any lawsuit threatens.

5

Repairs

RESIDENTIAL INCOME PROPERTY can be a great investment. However, the owner must be prepared, both financially and otherwise, to provide regular maintenance and all necessary repairs. If not, trouble will almost certainly arise.

This chapter addresses the following questions: What are the landlord's obligations? How about a tenant's obligations? What if the landlord fails to properly maintain the premises? What lease provisions are legal regarding repairs to residential rental property?

California law on this subject is very straightforward. One condition that can be legally included in a lease recites that the tenant has examined the premises prior to taking occupancy and has found everything to be in good working order. An itemized checklist should be attached to the lease. Another permitted clause prohibits repairs or alterations by the tenant without the landlord's prior written consent. (Remember, as I pointed out in Chapter 3, all security deposits are refundable. A nonrefundable deposit is illegal. Cleaning fees and all other deposits are considered a security deposit and this rule applies.)

A landlord is entitled to enter an apartment to make repairs or, presumably, to see if repairs are needed. According to law, however, this can only be done during normal business hours, and advance notice must be given. Written notice at least 24 hours in advance is recommended, except in a real emergency when earlier or immediate entrance may be required.

Under California law, if a landlord refuses to make repairs after a tenant has requested them, the tenant can hire someone to do the repairs and deduct the cost from the rent. The tenant's right in this regard cannot be waived, even by a written lease provision.

Tenants must keep the rental premises clean and sanitary, refrain from damaging or defacing them, and pay for whatever they or their guests break beyond normal wear and tear. Tenants must also allow the landlord entry to make needed repairs, to act in an emergency, and to show the property to a prospective tenant or purchaser.

What are a landlord's responsibilities? A landlord should advise tenants from the beginning that they should notify him or her immediately of any problem. Everything should be put in writing. The landlord should respond promptly to repair requests and have documentation of the prompt and appropriate action. A repair bill is usually the best evidence. All common areas outside the rental unit—for example, staircases—should be inspected regularly. Check with your insurance agent to verify that you have a comprehensive liability policy in case there is an accident.

State housing law requires the owner to have proper weatherproofing and waterproofing on all rental property. Plumbing, heating, and electrical systems must be maintained in good working order. Garbage receptacles must be provided and insect and rodent infestations controlled. Emergency exits must be free and clear and no combustible materials may be stored in the basement.

What can happen if a landlord fails to maintain the premises? As noted above, the tenants can do the repairs themselves or hire someone else to do them and deduct the repair costs from the rent. They can also withhold rent until the repairs are made. Either way, the landlord can expect that the building inspector will be called. The tenants can then successfully defend a nonpayment-of-rent eviction action. Moreover, the landlord may have to pay all the attorney fees. The tenants can also move out, even if they have a long-term lease. Or, in the worst case, they can sue the owner.

In conclusion, the best approach is strict compliance with all landlord responsibilities. From a trial attorney's viewpoint, it is a pleasure to represent someone who has complied fully with each of her responsibilities. If the tenant's case is unreasonable, it will be apparent to the judge or jury. If the landlord has done everything to maintain the high ground, morally and legally, it will not be difficult to prevail.

6

Tenants' Privacy

IN CALIFORNIA LAW, THERE IS ONE AREA of rental property ownership in which the rights of landlords and the rights of tenants can seriously overlap: A landlord's right to inspect rented premises is subject to the tenants' right to privacy. These overlapping rights are governed by a specific body of statutes and of *case law* (i.e., higher court decisions). In this chapter, we will identify both landlords' rights and tenants' rights, examining ways to handle the overlap between them.

California law guarantees tenants privacy in their dwellings. The law states that tenants are entitled to the *right of quiet enjoyment*. The law is very emphatic in this regard. If tenants' right to privacy is violated, they can actually sue their landlord for emotional distress. In fact, even if they are behind on their rent or are guilty of some other lease violation, tenants remain legally entitled to privacy.

What then are a landlord's rights? California law gives landlords the right to periodically inspect their rental property, but only for limited purposes. This is referred to legally as the *right to inspect*. Landlords may exercise this right in the following situations:

- ■ *To make necessary repairs.*

- ■ *To inspect for tenant damages when tenants are vacating a rental property. (If damage has been done, hopefully, you and your tenants can agree about appropriate deductions from the security deposit.)*

- ■ *To show the unit to potential tenants or buyers.*

- ■ *To inspect the property with new tenants to help uncover any dangerous or unsightly conditions, thereby avoiding future disagreements about the condition of the property if and when they take occupancy.*

- ■ *In the case of any emergency, when life or property are threatened.*

When a landlord and tenant have a congenial relationship, the landlord's right to inspect the property need not conflict with the tenant's right of quiet enjoyment. If both parties agree, inspections may take place at any mutually convenient time. If they do not have a congenial relationship, there are strict rules governing the landlord's right to conduct inspections. The courts will insist that a landlord adhere to them even if there are provisions in the lease to the contrary. Generally recognized procedures are:

1. Unless a landlord is entering the property because of an emergency in which life or property is threatened, the landlord must give *reasonable notice* to tenants about when he or she intends to carry out an inspection. Written notice given to tenants at least 24 hours in advance of the inspection is usually considered sufficient. In fact, in cases where landlords and tenants have ended up in court over these matters, this type of notice is considered the *established test of reasonableness*, meaning that the courts have usually ruled that the notice has been sufficient and the tenants' right to quiet enjoyment has not been violated, at least in this regard. Even with reasonable notice, though, it is important that a landlord does not abuse the right to inspect by doing so repeatedly or unnecessarily.

2. Inspections should be scheduled during normal business hours.

3. When property is up for sale and needs to be available for numerous inspections by potential

buyers, it is best to obtain weekly advance agreements with tenants on a schedule of times when the property will be shown.

Despite the potential for overlap between the landlord's rights and the tenants' rights, there are clear guidelines that make it possible for both parties to have their needs respected. So, when do problems arise? The worst scenarios are when landlords or their real estate agents (in the case of properties up for sale) are too aggressive in their inspection demands, or when tenants refuse to allow landlords to make the kinds of reasonable inspections described above. For landlords, the most difficult situation is when tenants change locks and do not provide them with new keys. To make sure you do not run into this situation, always include a provision in your leases or rental agreements stipulating either that locks not be changed, or that you be provided with duplicate keys if they are changed. If this situation occurs in a month-to-month tenancy and the necessary provision is not in the lease, serve your tenant with a Thirty Day Notice that the provision is going to be added.

Difficulties between landlords and tenants concerning a landlord's right to inspect his or her property and a tenant's right to privacy, or quiet enjoyment, can usually be worked out (unless, of course, either landlord or tenant is an unusually uncooperative person). If you have a proper reason for carrying out inspections, give tenants sufficient notice, and possess a passkey to the property, inspections should not be a problem. The best way a landlord can prevent problems is to maintain good communication and long-term positive relationships with tenants. If communication between landlord and tenant has been less than perfect, respectful and patient negotiations are usually the most fruitful approach to resolving conflicts.

Rent
Control

"*Good order
is the
foundation
of all things.*"

—Edmund Burke

*Reflections on the
Revolution in France,* 1790

7

Local Ordinances

S INCE THE MID-1970s, various communities in California, about 15 at last count, have enacted rent and eviction control laws. The strictness of these local ordinances varies widely. Berkeley and Santa Monica, for example, have a fairly radical form that requires the registration of all rental units and a virtual rent freeze even when units become vacant. (However, recent state law now mandates a phasing-out of the latter type of restriction.) Oakland and San Jose have a very relaxed structure that allows landlords generous rent increases. [See Appendix A.]

To make sure the laws have the intended effect, there are penalties to discourage violations. The penalties vary from city to city. The strict rent-control laws and even some moderate laws, such as those in San

Francisco, have misdemeanor criminal penalties, which means fines and possible jail time for violations. Other cities, such as Campbell, Cotati, and Los Gatos, have penalties that require either only a fine or no criminal consequences at all.

Most of these measures allow tenants to bring a civil suit for damages, such as the payment of excessive rent. These amounts can be tripled by the court at the time of judgment. San Francisco allows the tenant an award of attorney's fees, as well.

Many landlords violate local ordinances unknow-ingly. In San Francisco a rent increase can be made only once a year, at a rate measured by 60 percent of the annual cost-of-living increase. If an owner gets the per-centage wrong, or the anniversary date is off by a month or two, the increase can be denied. The consequences are even worse if the error is not discovered until years later: The rent board may rule all of the subsequent increases illegal and the owner will end up owing the tenant thou-sands of dollars.

Wrongful evictions can be much more serious. Using San Francisco as an example again, suppose a ten-ant is evicted so that the owner's daughter can move in. She does, but exactly one year later she moves out. (In San Francisco, in order to evict a tenant for an "owner move-in," the move-in must be for at least one year.) The landlord can be sued even if this minimum time frame has been met. So long as the eviction can be shown to have been for an ulterior purpose, the landlord can be liable after it is discovered. [See Chapter 21 regarding "owner move-ins."]

Criminal prosecutions for violation of rent and eviction control laws are fairly rare in California, perhaps because the civil penalties are rather serious. In addition to unfavorable rulings by the rent board, the consequences often rear their head in unlawful detainer cases. As noted earlier, if the annual rent increase was incorrect, even a landlord's suit against a tenant for nonpayment of rent might be defeated. Since the demand for rent was inaccurate, the tenant will win the case and can recover the attorney's fees as well. A landlord's violation of even unrelated or highly technical provisions of local law may jeopardize even legitimate proceedings. Thus, other types of evictions can be defeated on similar technicalities.

However, the big stakes involve an affirmative suit by a tenant for a rent refund or for wrongful eviction. Attorneys who bring these suits are usually highly specialized and are skilled at showing the owner's actions in the least favorable light. Juries often award handsome judgments and also require the landlord to pay the tenant's attorney's fees.

The simplest way for a landlord to avoid such problems is to obtain a copy of the current rent laws and rent board regulations from the local rent board office. [Refer to Appendix A.] Take your time reading them as they are usually somewhat technical. Most of the violations that I have seen have been the result of a lack of knowledge—simple ignorance. Even if a landlord is completely aware of all the provisions, interpreting their application in a given situation may be difficult. Fortunately, the staff at the rent board can often clarify matters, but their advice might also be biased at times in favor of the tenant. An attorney specializing in landlord-tenant law can be consulted for an experienced opinion, usually for a nominal charge. Then the owner will know all the correct procedures in advance and be aware of the possible consequences of violations. Making the effort to keep abreast of changes in the laws and regulations affecting one's rental properties might save many times the amounts one could be penalized for taking mistaken actions.

8 *Economic Impact*

IN CALIFORNIA THERE IS NO STATE-WIDE "rent control" law. While state law provides certain general rules regulating the landlord-tenant relationship—for example, the amount of security deposits a landlord may require—various California cities have specific laws that, for example, limit residential rents and require "just cause" for an eviction. ("Just cause" refers to a particular set of approved reasons for evicting a tenant under a local rent control ordinance, e.g., nonpayment of rent, nuisance, owner move-in. Chapter 9 has a discussion of "just cause.")

These laws not only vary considerably from city to city where they exist, they also change often. In addition, some housing within a community may be exempt for various reasons. Until a few years ago in San

Francisco, for example, a building of four units or less that was occupied by the owner was exempt from rent control laws. Even now, newly constructed units are not covered by the rent and eviction controls. Some laws even require owners to register their apartments and pay a fee for each unit that they own.

Several cities in California—Oakland, Hayward, San Jose, Los Gatos, etc.—have what might be called a "mild" form of rent control. Concerning the amount of rent that can be charged, these ordinances can best be described as "guidelines." They do not (except in Hayward) require a landlord to show "just cause" for eviction. The owner need only follow the procedures required by state law, typically beginning with a Thirty Day Notice to terminate a month-to-month tenancy.

A moderate form of rent control exists in the cities of San Francisco, Los Angeles, Beverly Hills, and Palm Springs. Here the rent increases are regulated by the local rent board and, typically, can be made only once a year in a very limited amount. Perhaps more important, a tenant cannot be evicted without "just cause." This means that the tenant can have an artificially low rent for an indefinite period—often for many years—unless the landlord can provide a very serious reason for displacing the tenant.

Fortunately for the landlord, the ordinances in these cities are of the "vacancy decontrol" type. When a tenant moves out, voluntarily or otherwise, the unit can then be rented at the market rate. Where the tenancy was long-term, the increase in rent is usually considerable.

The most severe type of rent control laws are found in the cities of Berkeley, Santa Monica, West Hollywood, East Palo Alto, and Cotati. These are the most extreme laws in that there is a "vacancy control" provision, which means that even if a tenant moves out, the maximum rent for the property does not go up. These laws also require "just cause" for an eviction. In addition, owners must register their rental properties with the local rent board which decides on the very small rent increase each year. A tenant can petition the rent board for a decrease in the rent if he can prove the property has not been properly maintained. As one might expect, owning income property in these communities is very unattractive. However, as mentioned earlier, vacancy decontrol is being phased-out statewide.

Courts, including the California and United States Supreme Courts, have, with minor exceptions, upheld the legality of these provisions. Thus, rent control comes down to a political decision based on the economic and social pressures that exist within the various communities. One researcher, an economist for the Federal Reserve Bank of San Francisco, made a study of the impact of severe rent control on residential properties. He noted that since tenants outnumber landlords in any given city, lawmakers and politicians tend to be more sensitive to tenants' concerns. As a result, housing decisions, such as rent control laws, are often based on political factors instead of market ones. He offered evidence to show that rent controls are economically dysfunctional in that they actually *increase* the cost of housing and reduce the supply. He suggested other remedies—such as encouraging renters to become owners—as a better solution.

Because tenants simply outnumber landlords, rent control laws are usually attractive to lawmakers. However, extreme forms of rent control can result in undermaintenance, abandonment and demolition. The experience in Europe since World War II, and in New York as well, indicates that new housing construction is discouraged by such protenant rent controls and that a better solution is to make ownership more available to the middle class.

9

Evictions Regulated

RENT CONTROL LAWS DO MORE than control rents. They also restrict evictions. Many cities in California have rent control and eviction regulations varying from mild to moderate to very strict in their provisions. San Jose, Oakland, Hayward, and Los Gatos, for example, have a form of "mild" rent control; Los Angeles, San Francisco, Beverly Hills and Palm Springs, a "moderate" version; and Berkeley, Cotati, East Palo Alto, Santa Monica, and West Hollywood, the most "strict" (some would even say oppressive). [These rent control ordinances are examined in Appendix A.]

The San Francisco rent control ordinance affects all rental units except those constructed or substantially rehabilitated since June 1979. It is considered moderate, at present, because it allows for "vacancy decontrol."

That means that if a unit becomes vacant, the landlord can raise the rent to a fair market rate, after which rent increases are once again subject to the rent control laws. In addition, the San Francisco ordinance requires "just cause" for eviction. This, in effect, allows the tenant a lifetime tenancy unless there is an allowable reason for eviction.

But what exactly constitutes "just cause"? "Just cause" evictions fall more or less into two categories: those based on the tenant's misconduct and those based on the landlord's legitimate needs. Examples of the former are: nonpayment of rent, violation of a clause of the lease, damage, and nuisance. They all permit an eviction even if there is a lease. Extensive remodeling as well as owner or relative move-in are common instances of the latter type of "just cause."

To effect an eviction, a landlord must first be able to prove the validity of the "just cause" reason and must comply also with a host of technicalities. Hiring a good lawyer is usually the best solution. But the landlord must fulfill certain basic requirements. For the curable breaches, such as nonpayment of rent or other lease violations, a proper Three Day Notice that allows the tenant a chance to correct the violation must be properly served on each occupant. Except in cases of nonpayment of rent, a copy of the notice should be mailed to the rent board. The detailed reason for the eviction must be specified on the face of the notice. In San Francisco, notification to the tenant must include both the fact that advice is available from the rent board as well as the local rent board's address and telephone number.

For a remodeling eviction (when the landlord intends to remodel the rental unit and can only do so if the unit is empty), the owner must first obtain all necessary permits from the city and must, in some cases, offer to pay the tenant's moving expenses. To evict a tenant so that an owner or owner's relative can move in, the name and relationship to the owner must be stated, and the percentage of the owner's interest in the rental unit and the date the ownership began must be disclosed.

As one might expect, eviction cases are often contested by the tenant. With vacancy decontrol in place, an evicted tenant often faces a substantial rent increase for his or her new home. And the fact that the unit will be decontrolled for a subsequent tenant can make an evictee suspicious.

Tenants' typical defenses include both attacks on the merits of an alleged "just cause" as well as more technical tactics. The latter are strict and numerous: For example, even a landlord's simple nonpayment of rent suit can be defeated if the landlord implemented even a slightly improper rent increase years before. The usual defenses to the merits of an eviction include a claim that the landlord's motive is retaliation against the tenant for some reason or another. A common rebuttal to an owner move-in claim is "ulterior motive"; that is, the tenant counterclaims that the landlord is merely trying to activate vacancy decontrol so that he or she can ultimately raise the rent.

Suffice it to say that, under these circumstances, a breach of the lease should be a major one and the other types of cases must be brought in good faith. If the owner loses, he may have to pay the tenant's attorney's fees. The owner may be sued as well and, of course, punitive damages can be awarded.

Antilandlord sentiment in rent-controlled cities is strong, and low-cost or free legal help is often available to tenants. Thus, many tenants who are threatened with eviction decide to stay and fight. For the property owner, it is often wiser to negotiate a settlement than to litigate, even in cases that seem to be a "sure thing." Litigation is expensive, and if the owner has perhaps violated the technicalities of a local ordinance, there are heavy penalties. In some cases, waiving a tenant's past-due rent or paying a tenant's moving expenses is a justifiable part of the settlement. A waiver provides certainty and relieves the anxiety of both parties. Furthermore, it is a more gentle (and thus desirable) way to do business.

Remember, however, to best avoid the whole litigation scene, take the necessary precautions: First, scrupulously check the credit and employment history of prospective tenants, and second, make sure you have the appropriate wrongful eviction insurance. After that, it is often luck and a positive attitude that determine how a landlord-tenant relationship will proceed.

SECTION THREE

Activities to Avoid

*"If one man can be allowed
to determine for himself what
is law, every man can.
That means first chaos,
then tyranny. Legal process
is an essential part of the
democratic process."*

—Felix Frankfurter, 1946

U.S. Supreme Court Justice

10 *Disrespecting Tenants*

THIS CHAPTER WILL EXPLORE three related aspects of the landlord-tenant relationship: activities that income property owners must try to avoid, actions a tenant can take if a landlord makes a mistake, and the best defense techniques an owner can use to protect his or her interests.

First, as was discussed in Chapter 1, landlords must avoid even the slightest hint of bias or discrimination against a tenant (or potential tenant) on the basis of race, gender, religion, national origin, marital status, or physical disability. A basic rule to remember is that any exclusion of a potential tenant that is not based on the owner's legitimate business needs is probably discrimination and thus illegal. (An exception applies if the owner occupies the rental premises and rents only a specified portion to a tenant.) No discrimination against a potential or actual tenant for the sole reason that the tenant has a child or children is permissible unless their occupancy would exceed the state or local occupant-to-space ratio.

Once a tenancy has begun, any number of situations might arise in which a landlord might offend a tenant. Even minor misunderstandings can develop into serious charges, such as improper entry, invasion of privacy, etc. The potential for offense is great, but most problematic situations can be avoided by the use of procedures that show your sensitivity to the tenant's privacy and legal rights in each case. If an inspection of the rental is necessary, for example, be sure to give the tenant written notice well in advance. If you must give a creditor or bank information about the tenant, be sure your report is accurate and unbiased. And, unless it is absolutely necessary, never contact a tenant at work.

If, despite these precautions, a situation becomes hostile, remember, a landlord is never justified for taking the law into his or her own hands. [See Chapter 12 about "self-help."] Finding a legal resolution to a tenant's claim that a landlord is guilty of harassment, threats, libel, or assault usually requires a lawyer's professional expertise and objectivity.

A responsible, thoughtful landlord will avoid the following scenarios which all involve liability:

■ *a lack of proper security,*

■ *a defective condition on the rental property which may cause an accident,*

■ *causing a tenant "mental distress," which is the typical claim in cases of harassment, threats, libel, assault, etc., and*

■ *"diminished habitability" of the rental property. (In these circumstances, tenants are advised to continue paying their full rent, suing the landlord for a partial refund.)*

Landlords should bear in mind that in the circumstances discussed here, the actions of any property managers—since they are the owner's agents—are deemed to be the actions of the owner.

Another type of tenant lawsuit involves charges of utility cutoffs or constructive eviction. Cutting off the heat, electricity, gas, water, or telephone of a tenant is sure to result in a claim for punitive damages. A landlord's greatest liability may result from a case of forcible, illegal, or retaliatory eviction, which usually involves the displacement of a tenant from a rent-controlled unit. (Occasionally, an owner's stated reason for an eviction is actually a ruse to get rid of the present tenant in order to rent the unit at market value to a new tenant. The former tenant must then also pay the market rate—sometimes hundreds of dollars more—for a comparable apartment. Should these facts be put before a court, the owner's liability in money damages will be considerable.)

Tenants can bring actions worth up to $5,000 in Small Claims Court. The most common case here is for the return of a security deposit after the tenants have vacated a rental unit. The general rule on security deposits is: The full amount—minus any unpaid rent or cost of repairs beyond reasonable wear and tear—must be returned to the tenant. The court may award punitive damages. In claims of harassment, tenants may seek a restraining order against the landlord or landlord's agent in Superior Court. For the more serious cases, such as personal injury or wrongful eviction, tenants can often obtain an attorney on a contingency (percentage) basis. In some jurisdictions, such as San Francisco, for an intentional wrongful eviction, the court must award punitive damages of at least three times the actual damages. Thus, if a tenant shows $25,000 in actual damages, another $75,000 in punitive damages would be awarded.

Sufficient and comprehensive insurance coverage is of vital importance to income property owners. In regard to the focal issues of this chapter, the policy should cover all potential claims by tenants of "illegal acts." Deal with a reputable insurance broker and ask for coverage for "wrongful eviction." Then, if sued, the insurance company must defend you. Usually, an insurance company hires a capable law firm to defend the suit

Disrespecting Tenants ■ 51

at no cost to the insured landlord. If the verdict or settlement goes against the owner, it is only in cases of "serious intentional wrongs" that an insurance company will
refuse to indemnify the landlord.

Finally, having represented numerous clients in
virtually all of the above described situations, I always
advise both landlord and tenant alike to exercise restraint
and show respect for each other. A landlord may say that
"it's my property," but it is the tenant's home. To obtain
the long-term benefits of ownership, a landlord must exe-
cute his or her responsibilities thoroughly and in a fair
and just manner. The most important time spent by a
landlord may be in learning about and purchasing an
appropriate insurance policy—just in case.

11 *Retaliation*

U NDER CALIFORNIA STATE LAW it is illegal to retaliate in any way against tenants for exercising their legal rights. Retaliation can take the form of a rent increase, a decrease in services, or an eviction. For example: A landlord, frustrated by tenants' continual demands for repairs to their apartment, evicts the tenants and claims a justifiable reason under a local rent control law (or gives no reason, which is allowed in a non-rent-controlled city). This eviction would be considered retaliation and is against the law.

California tenants have numerous legal rights in their relationship with a landlord. Tenants must be free of discrimination, must be allowed to complain to government agencies and courts, and must be provided with a rental space that is entirely suitable for habitation. A

California tenant may withhold rent if necessary repairs are not made, is entitled to privacy, and may sue a landlord for violating these or other rights.

Such legal protections would be meaningless, however, if the landlord could evict tenants for exercising those rights. Thus, it is illegal for a landlord or his agent to give a Notice to Quit [see Appendix D], to threaten to give a Notice to Quit, or to reduce services as retaliation. Even an otherwise valid rent increase may be invalid under certain circumstances, depending on the timing.

Another example: Some tenants organize a tenants' union to represent their interests against the landlord's, and the landlord suddenly decides to move his family into the apartment building. The courts would consider that a suspicious action and the landlord would be presumed to be retaliating. Because retaliation is against state law, it can be used by tenants' attorneys to defend such evictions anywhere in California, not just in rent-controlled cities like San Francisco.

Of course, sometimes a claim of retaliation is raised frivolously. If a tenant goes several months without paying rent, for instance, it would be absurd to claim that the landlord's Notice to Pay or Quit is done in retaliation. Nonetheless, this claim is often made, but is difficult to prove.

The timing of both the landlord's and tenant's actions is very important. If a rent increase or eviction attempt comes within 180 days after a tenant's complaint, state law presumes that the landlord is acting in retaliation. He must then prove otherwise. Even in a non-rent-controlled city where no reason is required to evict a tenant, a landlord may be better off providing one. In any case, there is always a reason, and if it is legitimate, the owner should not be afraid to state it. Examples of nonretaliatory reasons for evicting a tenant—whether in a rent-controlled area or not—are repeatedly late payments of rent, bad checks, nonpayment of rent, disturbing other tenants, or damaging the property. Other acceptable reasons would be the need to remodel the unit or the landlord's good-faith need to move into, or have a close family member move into, the apartment. Supportive evidence for the latter circumstance may be necessary—for example, the personal occurrences of the landlord or relative may justify his or her moving into that particular neighborhood at that particular time.

If a legitimate need to terminate a tenancy occurs at the same time a tenant is exercising his or her rights, the landlord must be very careful to stay within the law. A tenant's reasonable complaints, such as requests for minor or major repairs, should be honored. A reasonable "cooling off" period might also be observed, followed by a sincere letter to the tenant explaining the reasons why he or she must move. After these amiable preliminaries, the Notice to Quit may be served. Diplomacy often prevents hostilities and, in many cases, expensive litigation.

Deciding whether or not a landlord has acted in retaliation is the responsibility of a judge or jury. Much

depends on the history of the landlord-tenant relationship and the kind of impression both the tenant and the
landlord make in court. Each case is unique; most are
impossible to predict.

12 *Lockouts and Other "Self-Help"*

You have invested much time, money, and effort in the purchase and management of your income property, which you hope will be the means to achieve financial success. The last thing you want is to have your investment threatened by destructive or troublesome tenants. Therefore, if you experience difficulties with certain tenants, you may be tempted to bypass the standard legal measures and attempt to evict them as quickly as possible.

California law provides a number of specific eviction procedures. However, many eviction maneuvers that tempt property owners—known as "self-help"— are *illegal*.

Examples of "self-help" eviction maneuvers include:

■ *Locking tenants out of the property.*

■ *Removing or withholding tenants' personal belongings without a court order.*

■ *Shutting off tenants' utilities or allowing utilities of any kind to be shut off by ceasing to pay for them.*

■ *Threatening to take any of these actions.*

No matter how bad a tenant's behavior is or how tedious court procedures are, landlords are prohibited from taking any "self-help" shortcuts toward eviction. The courts will not enforce such actions—even if they are listed in the provisions of a lease. In fact, the law mandates serious penalties for property owners who engage in "self-help." To begin, you will probably be issued a *restraining order*: a court-enforced prohibition, such as an order not to approach the plaintiff-tenant or an order not to interfere with the tenant's activities. In addition, the police may be called to your property, an experience that has many negative consequences—not the least of which is bad publicity. Next, the tenant may file a civil lawsuit, and the courts will rule against you. You will be ordered to pay the actual damages that the tenant has suffered—e.g., expenses for hotel rooms, meals, etc.—plus an additional amount for emotional distress. Punitive damages—for example, a minimum of $100 per day for utility cutoffs—may also be added. All of these costs may tally up to a huge financial liability on your part. In one extreme case, a San Francisco landlord was ordered to pay $4.5 million to a group of tenants he had harassed.

There are two other serious consequences that can result from the use of shortcuts to induce an eviction. First, if you have a history of using "self-help" techniques, you may find it extremely difficult to evict a tenant in the future, even for legitimate reasons and even if you work within the court system. Second, you may face serious criminal prosecution for assault, battery, and trespass.

In sum, "self-help" is something you should avoid at all costs. But what other options are there for protecting one's real estate investment from problematic tenants? To understand your options, it helps to know about the notion of the *peaceful resolution of disputes*, one of our legal system's fundamental tenets. This concept entails resolving disputes through dialogue or the help of a neutral party (e.g., the courts, a mediator, etc.). The fact that "self-help" actions are directly opposed to the peaceful resolution of disputes is what makes them illegal. Of course, as I have stated repeatedly, one of the best ways to handle tenant problems is to avoid them in the first place by improving your management procedures, particularly the process of tenant selection [see Chapter 1, "Good Tenants"].

In addition:

1. Always treat tenants with respect.

2. Avoid personal confrontations with tenants whenever possible.

3. If you must enforce requirements, do so in a businesslike, matter-of-fact manner, preferably in writing.

4. If it is necessary to evict a tenant, use the court system to do so.

5. Finally, be sure to have adequate, comprehensive income property owner's insurance.

Following these guidelines will best protect your rental property investment.

13 *Wrongful Evictions*

IN THE 1970s, when local rent control laws were first adopted in parts of California, landlords became quite imaginative in evading them. In those cities where vacancies allowed landlords to raise rents to the current market rate, there was an incentive to evict tenants when their rental units increased in value. Amendments that mandated financial penalties were then enacted to close the legal "loopholes" that had enabled landlords to unscrupulously evict their tenants.

The allowance of an owner (or owner's relative) move-in was the most commonly abused privilege. If an owner or relative, who had successfully evicted a tenant under this provision, moved out shortly thereafter, the benefit of rerenting at the market rent was obviously to the detriment of the displaced tenant and to the great advantage of the owner. A similar misuse of a legitimate eviction proviso occurred in evictions based on a land-lord's alleged need to renovate. To counteract all such loopholes, tenants can now sue for all of their actual damages and collect punitive damages as well. Payment of the tenant's (in addition to his or her own) attorney's fees may be part of the loser's penalty. These provisions cannot be waived in the rental agreement.

If a tenant is evicted and believes that the eviction is not in compliance with the local rent law, the tenant has the right to sue the landlord for damages. This amount can be tripled by the court as additional damages to the tenant. In addition to paying the tenant's damages, a landlord has the expense of hiring an attorney to pre-sent his defense in the suit. (Thus, it is best to make sure you have insurance to cover this type of claim.) Since juries in cities that have rent control are usually made up mostly of tenants, factual disputes regarding whether or not the eviction was wrongful are often determined in favor of the tenant.

A rent increase is another issue that can subject a landlord to penalties if the increase violates a local ordi-nance. Even a closely restricted rent increase can be denied by the local rent board if needed repairs have been neglected. Also, an eviction for nonpayment of rent can be defended by the tenant's attorney if any technical requirement of the local ordinance has been overlooked or violated. In San Francisco, for example, certain refer-ences to the local law must be printed on the Three Day

Notice to Pay Rent or Quit form or the landlord will lose his case in court.

San Francisco's rent ordinance also permits denial of a rent increase and can require a rent *decrease* if the tenant presents evidence showing that housing services have been reduced. The San Francisco Rent Board itself may initiate a civil suit against a landlord to obtain punitive damages and attorney's fees if a court reaches a finding of wrongful eviction. The Rent Board can even recommend that a criminal proceeding be brought against the landlord by the District Attorney. Of course, the tenant is also likely to sue for this type of violation. The San Francisco ordinance defines a wrongful eviction as a landlord's failure to comply with the ordinance when: serving a Notice to Quit, making any demand that the tenant move, or filing an eviction action in court.

The potential financial damages, not to mention the anxiety and disgrace, are so serious that an income property owner must give serious consideration before proceeding with an eviction to ensure that adequate reasons exist and that all procedural requirements have been met. Only when such concerns are addressed and satisfied can a landlord proceed with confidence in removing a tenant.

Problems Along the Way

*"If you treat people right,
they will treat you right—
90 percent of the time."*

—Franklin D. Roosevelt, 1937

14

Changing the Terms of a Tenancy

THE TERMS OF A TENANCY specified in a rental agreement can only be changed by following certain rules. If the tenancy is on a month-to-month basis and *not* in a rent-controlled city, the landlord can make changes by the proper service of a Thirty Day Notice implementing the change. However, in a rent-controlled city, changes are very limited, and the owner must proceed very carefully. If the rental agreement deals with commercial premises, the property is exempt from rent control.

In the beginning, when a landlord and a tenant first negotiate a written lease, either or both may make changes. They can either cross out language or add any terms to which they agree. Each should initial these changes. Later, after the rental agreement has been signed and the tenant has taken possession, the parties may mutually agree on additional modifications. This should be done in writing either by adding an amendment to the original agreement or by signing a whole new contract. If the landlord wishes to make a change in a month-to-month tenancy to which the tenant does not agree, the landlord can make the change by serving the tenant with a Thirty Day Notice to Change Terms of the Tenancy. Note, however, that this is often not possible in a strict rent-controlled environment. The notice must be served properly [see Chapter 24].

A typical change to a rental agreement would be a rent increase. In a rent-controlled jurisdiction, the percentage of increase is usually limited and rent may only be raised once a year. Another change that landlords often make concerns the amount of security deposit. Note that this may be construed as an indirect rent increase and thus be prohibited under the rent control regulations. Under state law, a security deposit may not exceed two months' rent for an unfurnished apartment or three months' rent for a furnished apartment. Other changes, such as implementing house rules or restricting pets, are also possible. However, under rent control, these changes may be interpreted as indirect rent increases or a diminishment in housing services, which are issues that entitle a tenant to a Rent Board hearing and possible denial of the intended change.

Strict procedures govern the proper service of a notice to change the terms of a tenancy. A notice must be served on each tenant and personal delivery is preferred. The notice can be served at the tenant's residence or at his or her place of employment. If the occupant is not available at either location, a copy of the notice can be given to someone else who is there, and another copy should be mailed to the tenant who was not available. Finally, if no one is available to accept the notice at either the tenant's home or workplace, a copy for each tenant can be posted on the front door and another copy mailed to that person. The notice should name all of the occupants (if there are more than one), show their correct address, and state the effective date of the change—which must be at least thirty days after the date of service. Some authorities recommend adding an additional five days if the notice is mailed. The change to be implemented should be made very clear.

A rental agreement may also be changed verbally, although it is not recommended. A verbal change can be enforced only after the tenant has begun adhering to the stipulated change. In other words, once a tenant starts paying an increased rent, it evidences his or her agreement and the change is thereby executed. A change can also be proven by "reliance." In other words, if a landlord consistently accepts a tenant's late payments or accepts installment payments on a monthly rent, then the tenant can argue that the rental agreement has been changed to allow this form of payment.

A landlord is free to make changes to a rental agreement under the above circumstances. Changes may never be made, however, to retaliate against or harass a tenant for an activity such as requesting repairs. A change should only be made for a sound business purpose, and the change should be reasonable.

Property owners may serve a notice of change at any time during the month. Unless locally regulated, changes may also be made as often as is mandated by good business judgment. If all of these procedures are complied with and the above warnings are heeded, the owner has implemented a proper legal change that he or she can then rely on and enforce.

15

Breaking a Lease

A LEASE IS A LEGALLY BINDING agreement between a tenant and a landlord that describes the conditions under which the tenant may occupy a property owned by the landlord. One of the main conditions contained in all leases is the length of time that the agreement will last. This time period is known as the *term* of the lease. Neither the landlord nor the tenant has the legal right to terminate a tenancy based on a lease before its term expires unless the other party violates some other lease condition. Nonetheless, it often happens. In this chapter, I will describe the four most common scenarios in which leases are broken, and also what a landlord can do when they occur.

1. The tenants give notice that they are moving before the lease terminates.

Theoretically, a tenant can be held responsible for all of the rent that is due for the duration of the term of his or her lease. California law, however, imposes what is known as a *duty to mitigate* on the landlord. This term means that, before collecting the lease's remaining rent from a departing tenant, the landlord must try to find a replacement tenant at the same rent for which the departing tenant was responsible. If the landlord is able to do this and a new tenant moves in, the rent the new tenant pays is deducted from the amount of rent the departing tenant owes. In this case, the departing tenant does not necessarily lose all the security deposit, but is responsible for paying the lost rent and landlord's cost of advertising for a replacement tenant.

Let's say, for example, that the departing tenants gave notice and then moved out with three months left to go on their lease. If replacement tenants move in for the last two months of the original lease term and pay the same monthly amount of rent that the original tenants were obligated to pay under the lease, then the departing tenants will only owe rent for the one month that the property is vacant. Thus, the departing tenants are legally required to pay the unpaid rent under their lease, minus rent received (or that could have been received) from a new tenant, minus their security deposit, and plus the landlord's cost of advertising.

In a variation of this scenario, the departing tenant may locate a replacement. What is the owner's responsibility now? The owner has the same duty. He must cooperate and should only reject the proposed occupant—whether a subtenant or a replacement—on the basis of their poor financial standing or poor tenancy history.

2. The tenants simply disappear.

Your first indication of this scenario may be when the rent is not paid on time. If it seems that the tenants are gone and the rent has not been paid for at least 14 days, you can serve the tenants by mail with a Notice of Belief of Abandonment. If they do not respond within the next 18 days, you can legally change the locks of the property, and possession of the apartment will then belong to you. If the tenants left personal possessions behind, you must mail the tenants another notice called a Notice of Right to Reclaim Abandoned Property. You must also include or attach a list of the possessions left behind. The tenants then have 18 days to recover their possessions. Although you are entitled to charge them reasonable storage costs during this time, you may find it better to simply release their possessions to them and thus solve the problem without further dispute.

3. One tenant departs, but a roommate, who then brings in a replacement tenant, remains.

These circumstances give rise to many questions about assignment and subleasing (some of which are addressed in Chapter 16, "Subtenants Becoming Tenants"). The departing tenant, however, can still be held responsible if those staying on fail to pay the rent.

4. A tenant dies.

When a tenant dies, delicate questions arise concerning the disposition of his or her personal belongings which are in the rental property. If you act improperly in such cases, you could become liable for *wrongful disposition* of the belongings. Therefore, you should be careful about allowing anyone, even a family member, to remove anything from the property because landlords are not allowed to judge how the deceased's estate will be distributed. The only exception to this rule is if the tenant's spouse survives; a spouse is the one relative who may make decisions about what to do with the deceased's personal property. Otherwise, a Probate Court order is the surest method to relieve a landlord from any potential liability for the wrongful disposition of the deceased tenant's belongings.

We have now taken a look at the four main scenarios in which tenants sometimes terminate a lease before its term expires, and have considered some of the best ways to handle each of them. In addition to these solutions, you might also be tempted to recover the rent lost through early termination by suing the tenants who have walked out on their lease. I do not recommend this approach: It is usually of little practical use. Not only may it be difficult to track down such tenants, but also, because the demand for residential property in California is generally high, a replacement tenant can usually be found with reasonable effort. Only where the rent is high and the demand is low is a lawsuit to recover lost rent recommended.

16 *Subtenants Becoming Tenants*

Most residential and commercial rental agreements require the landlord's prior written consent before the tenant can assign or sublease to another tenant. "Assigning" a tenancy means the tenant leaves and gives over his entire tenancy rights to someone else. "Subleasing" means the tenant gives part of his rights—such as part of his living space—to another.

For various reasons, it is important that a landlord know who is physically occupying the rental property. Is the new person qualified? Is he or she responsible? In areas with rent control laws, the landlord may be denied a reasonable rent increase even after the original tenant has vacated. This situation happens because a subtenant now becomes an "original tenant" and thus qualifies for the rent control that would have become inapplicable after the actual "original tenant" vacated. This is the real economic battle often involved in sublease disputes.

If the new occupant qualifies as an "original tenant" under the local rent control ordinance, it can cost the landlord a lot of money because a landlord can raise the rent to market level when an original tenant moves out under the usual form of rent control. But if the newcomer is allowed to merge into the arrangement as a tenant, the new person will be allowed to pay the same rent until he or she vacates. Sometimes this situation denies the landlord several thousand dollars per year in additional legitimate rent. This tenant can then stay on virtually forever at the artificially and unfairly deflated rental amount.

How do these situations occur? How can a landlord spot such a thing before it is too late? Tenants have a right to have a guest, a roommate, a lover, a spouse. Unless they are overcrowding the unit, against the local health laws, there is not much a landlord can do. A landlord has a right, however, to know who is occupying his or her property and can politely inquire. A landlord is also allowed to make periodic, modest rent increases if the lease provides—even under rent control. But it is very important for a landlord to be aware if an original tenant leaves. When a roommate stays on, he or she sometimes continues to pay the rent with the former tenant's checks for the purpose of concealing the facts from the landlord. Commonsense efforts, such as calling the apartment and asking for the original tenant, may indicate whether or not that person has vacated. Asking the residential property manager or a neighbor may also help, as will a call to the original tenant's workplace.

How can you avoid all this? First, never take a rent payment from anyone other than the original tenant. If you do, you may be legally bound to accept the new person as a tenant. Second, give your original tenant and any newcomers a written notice stipulating that when the last original tenant vacates, a new tenancy is automatically created for the purpose of setting the rent. (The San Francisco Rent Board regulation, Section 6.14, addresses this point.)

If you suspect that a newcomer is trying to become a tenant, ask to see the original tenant and request the identity of all other occupants. If you cannot find the original occupant, you may conclude that he or she has gone and left new people behind. You may then seek their legal removal, even under rent control, as unapproved subtenants.

There are limits, however, to what a landlord can do in this situation. You cannot lock out unauthorized occupants nor can you call the police, claiming the occupants are "trespassers." They are not trespassers since they gained possession peacefully, even though it was without your consent. You cannot harass them nor neglect their rights as tenants in any way. If a court decides they are not tenants, the sheriff will enforce that judgment and put them out. Prior to that time, you should treat them like your other tenants, while at the same time asserting your rights in court.

Sometimes the landlord-tenant relationship seems like economic warfare. All is fair, it is said, in love and war. As a result, trickery and deceit are often employed to gain advantage. But if the landlord acts responsibly and with concern for the rights of his tenants, he or she can maintain the ethical as well as the legal "high ground." And when a would-be tenant attempts an unlawful scheme to establish occupancy, it will be possible to expose it and to defeat it. Your own vigilance to protect your rights and the retention of expert legal counsel will serve you well.

Reasons for Terminating a Tenancy

"Through the centuries,
men of law have been persistently
concerned with the resolution
of disputes...in ways that enable
society to achieve its goals
with a minimum of force
and maximum of reason."

—Archibald Cox, 1973

17 *Late-Paying Tenants*

LANDLORDS DEPEND ON TIMELY RENT payments to meet their own obligations. But tenants sometimes ignore their obligation to pay the rent on time. What can a landlord do about it?

First, let us define our terms. If a tenant's rent is overdue, it is actually a nonpayment-of-rent situation. Serve the tenant a Three Day Notice. If the rent is paid within the notice period, or if it is paid before you get around to serving a notice, it is a late-payment case.

If there is no lease involved, you can terminate the tenancy by properly serving a correctly worded Thirty Day Notice to Terminate, making sure to name all the occupants. If there is a lease, you cannot serve a Thirty Day Notice to Terminate until the lease expires and it becomes a month-to-month tenancy.

If the tenancy is commercial, or if it is residential but without rent control, you do not need to give a reason for the termination. But within a rent control jurisdiction, such as San Francisco, you must state the reason—e.g., the consistently late payment of rent—on the notice. There are several other technical elements required in the notice, as well.

In a rent control area, a nonpayment-of-rent case is much easier to win than a late-payment one. Nonpayment is a straightforward fact while late payment is more subjective. (How late is late?) Therefore, it is best to continue to serve Three Day Notices whenever rent is late. If the tenants do not comply within the notice period, proceed to court.

If rent has been paid for the current month but is regularly late, or if bad checks are often given, and if there is a lease, you may be stuck. Nevertheless, serve a Three Day Notice every time the tenants are late, and you will either get them to change their ways or, one of these times, you will have a nonpayment-of-rent case. Make sure the notice is properly and personally served. [Refer to Chapter 24, "Correct Service of a Notice."] These efforts eliminate legal delays.

If the tenancy is on a month-to-month basis, you can terminate it with a Thirty Day Notice. For commercial tenancies and non-rent-control residential tenancies, no reason need be given. But termination must not be motivated by any retaliatory intent. These types of cases should be quite simple. However, the tenant usually will not be out at the end of 30 days and so you will need to proceed to court. Remember, you cannot just change the locks.

If the premises are under a residential rent control ordinance, such as exists in San Francisco, a late-payment-of-rent eviction is possible. But do not try it unless you have a strong case. The tenant will have a strong motivation to stay and fight, especially if the rent is low and way below the market rate.

The tenant may also have a legitimate basis of defense. For example, if the tenant does not have an extremely bad rent payment history, the landlord will appear to have an ulterior motive—such as simply wanting to get rid of a low-paying tenant. The tenant can also claim that the landlord has continually accepted late payments without protest and so has waived his right to prompt payment.

There are ways open to a landlord to overcome these defenses, but a jury, if the case goes that far, can be quite sympathetic to a tenant in this situation. If there is any strength to the landlord's case, he or she should be able to negotiate a move-out agreement. Does the tenant need more time? Then give it to him. But get the move-out settlement in the form of a judgment that the sheriff will enforce if need be.

Most important, carefully evaluate a case of late payment before you act, or you may have a big legal bill and nothing to show for it. If you think you have a reasonably strong case, measure the costs versus the benefits. If you win, but it costs you too much, did you really win? If there is a good chance of losing, and losing expensively, is it a wise decision to proceed? To properly analyze each unique situation, find a qualified attorney whom you can trust.

18

Breach of Covenant

A LANDLORD LOSES HIS RIGHT to receive rent if he breaches the covenant to provide decent housing. Similarly, tenants may forfeit their rights, including the right to occupy the rental unit, if they fail to pay rent or uphold other obligations of the lease. Some lease terms, known as "covenants," are not enforceable as matters of law. Others are not worth pressing for practical reasons. Many can and should be upheld, for the sake of the building and the other people who occupy it.

Examples of lease terms that *cannot* be enforced by the landlord are the prohibition of waterbeds (there is a California statute on the subject) and the waiver of certain rights by the tenants, such as the duty of the landlord to give notice before inspection. Limiting the number of persons who can occupy a unit, or restrictions on subletting, can also be tricky. Terms that *can* be enforced by the landlord are: the implementation of reasonable late charges, payment of security deposits, prohibition of pets, violation of any public laws, and rules and regulations regarding the behavior of the tenants in common areas. Even strict rent and eviction control ordinances do allow evictions based on such a breach of covenant but sometimes a prior warning is required before the service of the first notice. If the covenant in question was added after the original lease was signed, this may present special problems.

Under California law, the procedure to enforce lease terms begins with a Three Day Notice to Perform Covenant or Quit. This can even be done during a one-year lease. The notice must be properly served on all known occupants, with their precise names and the addresses on the notice. The clause of the lease at issue and the alleged violation must also be spelled out in detail so that the tenant understands what the problem is and how he or she might cure the breach. If the violation is not corrected by the time the notice expires (eight days instead of three days if it was not served personally), an Unlawful Detainer lawsuit can be filed. This usually requires the services of an attorney who specializes in the field. If the tenant contests the case, a trial will be required. Unless the parties can find a settlement, which will be encouraged by the court, the landlord has the burden of proof to obtain a judgment.

Local rent control ordinances, such as San Francisco's "Rent Stabilization and Arbitration Ordinance," also require that the notice inform tenants that advice is available to them from the Rent Board. Failure to properly draft this document will defeat any court action based on it.

In addition to a host of technical defenses that are usually brought up by defendants in Unlawful Detainer suits, a tenant can assert substantive defenses as well. Common defenses include the concept of "waiver" if the landlord has somehow allowed—either expressly or implicitly by his action—the breach to continue in such a way that the lease term at issue is no longer enforceable. If the breach is trivial, the tenant can also win. For example, if the breach of covenant is based on a claim that the tenant has broken the law, and this allegation is based on a single marijuana cigarette having been seen in the apartment, this would probably not be enough for the owner to prevail. Also, if rent is accepted after the notice is served, this would constitute reinstatement of the tenancy, and the landlord would lose. And, if it can be shown that the landlord is retaliating against the tenant or, under local law, that he or she has some type of ulterior motive, this can be a complete defense.

If a tenancy is not in a rent-control jurisdiction and if it is on a month-to-month basis, it is much simpler to terminate: Just give a Thirty Day Notice. Even here, however, it is best to state a reason so that the notice cannot be construed as retaliation for some legitimate act of the tenant. There is much less to prove in these cases and defenses are almost nonexistent. However, to win a breach of covenant case in court, the landlord's proof needs to be convincing; in other words, the misconduct claimed must be serious enough that a judge or jury will want to order the tenants removed. Other tenants or the tenant's neighbors have the most credibility. Their involvement makes the lawsuit, in effect, a case of tenants versus an inconsiderate tenant, allowing a judge or jury to more easily conclude that the offending defendant-tenant should be evicted.

19

The Nuisance Tenant

IN THE BIG-BUDGET HOLLYWOOD MOVIE *Pacific Heights*, filmed in San Francisco, Meg Ryan and Matthew Modine play a couple who learn the hard way how a criminal tenant can victimize a landlord, destroy a lovely property, and terrorize neighbors. I have seen it happen in real life, and it is not pretty. How does a landlord terminate such a tenancy?

The first step in both unregulated and rent-controlled jurisdictions is a Three Day Notice to Quit [see Appendix D]. This document must be prepared and served whether or not the tenant has a written lease. Some tricky technicalities in the text as well as the method of service are involved in the implementation of this document. Thus, it might be wise to consult a professional. Although an attorney can ensure that the details are covered, retaining legal aid may depend upon the aggrieved landlord's assessment of the situation.

Will the tenants resist eviction? If so, then an Unlawful Detainer lawsuit must be filed in court, and a summons must be served on the resisting tenants. If they fail to respond to the summons within five days, the landlord wins by default and the sheriff will enforce the judgment within a matter of weeks.

If, however, the tenants decide to fight the lawsuit, the property owner or manager must be prepared to persuade a judge or jury that the occupants are truly undesirable. First, a winning strategy must be chosen. Although seemingly more costly than doing the eviction oneself, hiring a lawyer who specializes in the field is usually a good investment. Mistakes made by a novice can result in setbacks of weeks and months or, ultimately, even defeat.

Other tenants and neighbors are often the key to victory. Their testimony about the bad habits, loud noises late at night, possible illegal activities such as drug dealing in common areas, etc., is crucial. Anything that pertains to the bothersome tenant's general disregard for the comfort and well-being of other residents will resound in court.

It may often be difficult to prove that tenants have damaged physical property. The old "That was like that when I arrived" is a typical rejoinder. But if witnesses back up the landlord's claims, the defendant will get scant sympathy from a judge or jury. In fact, the very presence of witnesses may intimidate tenants who plan to base their defense on fabrications.

Some troublesome tenants will want to steer clear of court entirely. So it is important to assess the possibilities early. If a tenant proves court-shy, the landlord will most likely win by default or be able to ease the tenant out with a minor concession—e.g., waiving some overdue rent or permitting a short grace period for the tenant to vacate the premises. Nonetheless, it is important to have the judgment enforceable by the sheriff, in case the tenant is all-talk and no-walk.

Another factor that a landlord must consider is how to cover the expenses incurred from dealing with a problematic tenant. Insurance companies generally will not recompense an owner for lost rent, attorneys' fees, or court costs. But they will often cover costs to repair damage resulting from vandalism. Make sure you keep detailed records of monies spent, and use photographs, if possible, to illustrate your case.

As I have mentioned numerous times in this book, the best way to extricate yourself from unpleasant situations is to avoid them in the first place:

■ *Scrutinize the applications of potential tenants.*

■ *Develop antennae to pick up the "flake factor."*

■ *Phone previous landlords.*

■ *Check credit references and employment history.*

■ *Call their bank to see if there is enough in the account to cover the deposit and rent required.*

Once tenants move in, monitor their occupancy. Have others moved in on the sly? Make regular inspections, but give the tenants 24 hours' notice, in writing. [See Chapter 6, "Tenants' Privacy," regarding the appropriate procedures for inspections.] Privacy laws hamper landlords here, but routine pest control servicing, plumbing inspections, etc., can provide legitimate means for regular entrance. Then take the opportunity to get a good gander at the place. If you do not like what you see, move swiftly. The longer you wait, the more difficult the eviction process may be and the more damage the property may sustain.

20

A
Landlord's
Right to Remodel

MANY RENT CONTROL ORDINANCES, including San Francisco's, allow an eviction for the landlord's extensive remodeling of a rental unit. Prior to an eviction of this nature, the landlord must satisfy certain requirements, including these stipulations: The tenancy is month-to-month, all permits for the remodeling work have been secured, and a proper Thirty Day Notice to Terminate [see Appendix D] has been correctly served on all occupants of the unit. The work must be so substantial that the tenants cannot be physically present, and the work must be completed within a reasonable time.

In San Francisco, for example, there are two very distinct methods for a remodeling eviction. One type, known as "capital improvements," is less burdensome on the landlord and does not affect the tenant's occupancy rights. The other type, which is based on "substantial rehabilitation," is more difficult to qualify for, but results in a removal of the building from rent ordinance restrictions.

Capital Improvements

The eviction for capital improvements in San Francisco has the following specific requirements: The plans must be on file with the Permit Bureau; the tenants must be informed that they can inspect those plans; the tenants must be allowed back within three months (with possible extensions); and moving costs of up to $1,000 per adult must be paid.

After the tenants have returned, they pay their former monthly rent plus a "pass through"—a portion of the capital improvements' cost paid over a period of years. Of course, the tenant is not required to resume the tenancy and may choose to stay in his or her new location. The potential for this situation often arises during the eviction proceedings. The tenants, under certain negotiated circumstances, can stipulate not to return. However, the agreement must be carefully worded to avoid violation of local law. Most rent control laws prohibit a buy-out of tenant rights.

Substantial Rehabilitation

Substantial rehabilitation of a unit in San Francisco allows an eviction in which the tenants are not given the

right to return to the rental unit, unless they are willing to pay a new rent based on the current market. In these circumstances, the financial commitment of the owner must be great. The structure must be 50 or more years old, and the cost of the rehabilitation must be 75 percent of replacement value of the building, excluding land costs. In addition, the structure must be virtually uninhabitable because of health and safety violations, and the reconstruction must be extensive and not just cosmetic.

Because tenants under San Francisco's rent control laws have a virtual lifetime tenancy, there is often a strong motivation to stay and fight if an owner's renovation plan displeases them. Many times, the courts defeat an eviction for a landlord's failure to comply with seemingly minor technical requirements. For example, a single outdated permit may result in the tenant prevailing. Also, if a notice to vacate is served within six months of a tenant complaint, there is a legal presumption that the eviction is retaliatory. This presumption can be overcome, but it is not easy. Given the obvious financial advantage to a landlord of getting rid of a low-paying tenant, the court will sometimes suspect that the landlord has an ulterior motive. Generally, if the tenant wins an eviction trial, he or she will subsequently sue the landlord. Such outcomes are one reason that owner/landlords should be sure to have the right type of liability insurance before beginning such a legal project.

Because antilandlord sentiment and attorneys' fees are high, when an important development project is at stake a negotiated result is often better for all parties. A waiver of rent owed and moving expenses are usually the minimum considerations. Each case is different, but the advantages of relieving anxiety and uncertainty, reducing litigation costs, and preserving an amicable landlord-tenant relationship often recommend the negotiated settlement. Once both parties reach an agreement, an experienced attorney should draft the written document to insure its validity and enforceability.

Finally, make sure all the financial plans as well as the arrangements with contractors are in place before commencing an eviction. The reason is that once the owner succeeds in removing the tenants—whether by negotiation or by court order—it is very important that the remodeling work begins promptly and is completed on time. If not, the owner may encounter more legal problems in addition to the rising financial costs.

21 *The Owner Move-in Case*

AN OWNER OF A RENTAL PROPERTY may encounter a situation in which he or his relatives may need to move into a unit of his property even though tenants currently reside there. On one hand, the owner has certain rights of ownership, including the fundamental right to occupy one's own property. On the other hand, tenants have rights—particularly with the advent of rent and eviction control laws—that protect them from arbitrary displacements. These two seemingly opposing principles clash in the case of an "owner move-in," which will be examined in this chapter.

The right of "ownership" has always been limited. While one might claim "but I own it," the reality is usually somewhat different. Quite frequently, the bank owns 80 or 90 percent of the building, and the government has the right to tax the building. Moreover, rent-paying tenants, who have a right to occupancy, often make it possible for the landlord to pay the mortgage so he can remain the "owner." Certainly, there are numerous benefits to real estate ownership, but there are many limitations as well—partly because of rent and eviction ordinances, which give additional rights to tenants and limit the power of the owner.

Although they vary from city to city, a typical local rent ordinance normally aims to keep the rents artificially low and to limit evictions. In order to proceed with an eviction in San Francisco, for example, a landlord must have "just cause." Typically, provisions permitting an eviction can be divided into two categories: those that focus on the bad behavior of a tenant and those that focus on the convenience of the landlord. The most typical of the latter category is the "owner move-in" eviction: a displacement of a tenant so that the landlord or a member of the landlord's family can occupy the evicted tenant's unit.

There are serious technical requirements to implement an owner move-in eviction. The definition of an owner must first be checked under the pertinent ordinance and any regulations that have been passed pursuant to it. Under San Francisco law, for example, a landlord in an owner move-in case must have at least 50 percent interest in the property (if acquired after February 21, 1991). Typically, the owner must be an individual rather than a corporation or partnership. The definition of a "relative" under the laws must also be checked. Most often, a parent or child of an owner will qualify. And under some ordinances, including San Francisco's, the grandparents, grandchildren, brothers, sisters, or the spouse of those relatives will also qualify.

Another key term pertinent to a move-in eviction is "comparable unit." If another unit in the building or in another building owned by the same landlord is available and is similar to the one in question, the landlord or his relative will be expected to move into this "comparable unit." This requirement is part of the San Francisco Rent Ordinance. Additional technical requirements govern the content of the notice to vacate and the method by which the notice is served on the occupants.

Typically, the owner must also be prepared to prove that he is seeking this particular unit as a *permanent* and *primary* residence for himself or for his relative. He must be acting in "good faith," and his stated reason must be his "dominant motive." Timing is very important: The eviction must not in any way appear to be in retaliation against the tenants for exercising any of their legal rights. Note that if, under rent control, the current rent of the unit in question is below the market rate, the Rent Board or the courts may suspect that the owner's "dominant motive" is to displace the tenant so that the rent can be raised to the market level, thereby creating a windfall for the landlord. This and other commonsense tests will be applied by the judge or jury reviewing a move-in eviction.

The court will consider carefully, for example, background information pertaining to the person(s) intending to move into the evicted tenant's space. Many questions will be asked:

- *Where does the owner or the proposed relative live now?*

- *Where does he or she work or go to school?*

- *What size apartment does the person occupy in relation to the size of the desired unit?*

- *What is the rental level of other units in the building and in any other building owned by the same landlord?*

- *What has the relationship between this tenant and the landlord been up to this point?*

In the early years of rent control, many owner move-in provisions were often abused. Amendments were then passed which now allow tenants to collect money damages, including extra "punitive" damages, for violations. If tenants can prove that they were wrongfully evicted, they can be awarded attorney's fees. Thus, many tenants' attorneys are eager to hear about an alleged wrongful eviction. And in most wrongful eviction cases, attorneys also include claims for intentional and negligent infliction of emotional distress. I strongly advise landlords to act in good faith and to verify that they have adequate insurance to cover this type of lawsuit; however, even insurance companies will not cover claims if a landlord acts with the intent to violate the law.

Be aware that a tenant could be acting very cleverly when he suspects some wrong-doing. After meekly moving out as he is requested to do, the tenant could then investigate the situation six or 12 months later. If he then discovers that the owner or relative no longer resides there, the tenant may initiate a major lawsuit against the landlord.

If the tenant claims that a proposed owner move-in is illegal, the landlord should retain a competent attorney experienced in this field. Then, together, they can consider what might look suspicious to a jury. After having analyzed all the elements of the case, they should consider the cost in attorney's fees for a trial, as well as the anxiety, stress, and the possibility of ugly accusations being made. After a careful evaluation of the situation, a landlord should seriously consider the positive aspects of reaching an out-of-court agreement with the tenant. Giving the tenant extra time and, possibly, moving expenses, are effective components of an out-of-court settlement. However, the agreement should show a specific move-out date. If the agreement is properly drawn up and filed with the court, the sheriff will definitely enforce it. The best aspects of this solution are the certainty of recovering the unit in question for the use of the owner and his family as well as the avoidance of a potentially expensive and lengthy legal battle.

How to Terminate a Tenancy

"I have always found that mercy bears richer fruits than strict justice."

—Abraham Lincoln, 1865

22 *The General Rules*

THIS CHAPTER COVERS THE BASIC RULES for terminating a tenancy under California law. It does not address the additional requirements of local residential rent laws of some cities, such as San Francisco. However, it explains the different ways of terminating a tenancy, both a month-to-month tenancy and those governed by a lease for a term such as six months, a year, or more. Note that under certain circumstances, both tenants and landlords can terminate a tenancy.

Some cities in California have a tough set of special requirements to terminate a residential tenancy. These requirements are in addition to the general provisions of state law. But even without local laws, there are factual as well technical conditions that must be met to successfully remove a tenant. And even if a landlord meets all such conditions, the courts and the sheriff must be used. "Self-help" is prohibited [see Chapter 12]. There are civil and criminal penalties for landlords who violate this rule.

Terminating a Month-to-Month Tenancy

Known as a "periodic" tenancy, this type of tenancy lasts for the duration of the rent payment period (usually one month). An eviction of a "periodic" tenant is not complicated. A properly written notice, correctly naming the occupants and describing the premises, must be served. In the case of a monthly tenancy, it must be served at least 30 days in advance of the termination date. A clear intention to terminate the tenancy, unconditionally, must be stated.

Although there is always a reason to terminate, the reason need not be stated. A landlord should be especially cautious if the notice to terminate is within six months of a tenant complaining about something. As long as the termination is not an act of retaliation against the tenant for exercising legitimate rights, the termination should be successful.

Terminating a Lease Tenancy

Absent a local rent control law, a lease for a term ends automatically at its termination date. Terminating a lease for a term, such as a one-year lease, is more difficult than ending a month-to-month tenancy before its termination date. There must be a stated reason: Usually, there has been a breach of a covenant or rule by the tenant. It must be an important breach, and the tenant must be given a chance to "cure," or remedy, the breach. A Three Day Notice "to perform the covenant or quit" must be served [see Appendix D]. If the tenant fights the termination, the landlord must prove that a covenant was broken. Nonpayment of rent is the most common offense, and usually the easiest to prove. Other breaches, such as sub-leasing or failing to maintain the premises, are more difficult, as the facts are often complicated. The court's possible sympathy for the tenant may also come into the picture. Attempting to terminate a lease tenancy because a tenant has violated a no-pet rule, for example, might be a tough case. Think of all the pet lovers who may be on the jury.

Many landlords get off to a faulty start in trying to end a tenancy by inaccurately filling out and/or serving a notice (usually a Thirty Day Notice). Name all the adult occupants, including any known subtenants. Get the address right, too. All named occupants should get a copy. Personally putting the notice into each person's hands is best. If you cannot serve them at home or at work, you can mail them a copy and also leave a copy for them with a co-occupant. As a last resort, you can post copies on their door and mail one to each occupant. First-class mail is sufficient for this option. Or, for a Thirty Day Notice, you can mail the notice by using certified mail without also posting copies on the door. This notice may be served at any time during the month. Note: Do not accept any more rent after serving the notice.

Landlords should be cautious, especially when already upset by a tenant. Always be courteous: Anything you say or do can be construed against you. A competent attorney familiar with this field can be your best friend, saving you money, time, and frustration. The process of eviction—putting someone out of their residence—is a unique type of legal action, and the law requires the owner to comply with all the procedures. Delays are common, especially when a tenant takes the case to court. The more carefully you prepare and the more you comply with all legal requirements, the less delay and frustration there will be.

23

Typical Evictions

HAVE YOU EVER NEEDED TO EVICT A TENANT? Whether you actually went through with the eviction or not, you were probably left with many unanswered questions. Given the unpleasantness and expense of that experience, you probably hope to avoid similar situations in the future.

There are several situations that commonly necessitate an eviction: nonpayment of rent, a nuisance tenant, and a need for the owner's relative to move in. Nonpayment cases are often reasonably simple if handled correctly. Nuisance cases can be winners, too, if the court feels that the tenants are really as undesirable as the landlord says they are. Owner or relative move-in cases can be the most delicate and the most expensive.

If a tenant is not paying the rent because he does not have it, the landlord will almost always prevail in court. Even if the tenant proves that the apartment is not in perfect condition, the court will require the tenant to pay at least a portion of the rent. This is one of the few situations in which it is quite predictable that the landlord will prevail. If the tenant does not have the rent, he or she will be evicted. There are many technical details to be covered, however, to effect the eviction, and your attorney must be familiar with them all.

A nuisance case can be brought if a tenant, though paying the rent, is either disturbing other occupants or damaging the property. Calling the police can help, but the landlord must still go through the civil courts for an eviction, even if the tenant is arrested. The best way to win this type of case is to have as many other tenants as possible ready to testify how unbearable the tenant's behavior is. Otherwise, the tenant can claim that the plea of "nuisance" is all in the imagination of the landlord.

Owner or relative move-in cases will work, in rent-control jurisdictions, if they are legitimate. If the landlord is actually simply fed up with the tenants for some reason, however, a judge or a jury can easily spot it. And, if the eviction case is lost, the landlord can then be sued by the tenant. The tenant can also sue if the owner or relative never moves in or fails to stay for a sufficient period. Landlords should have the right type of insurance policy if they intend to implement an owner or relative-move-in eviction.

How long will the eviction take? How much will it cost? The Three or Thirty Day Notice is only the first step. The court procedure adds another month, even if the tenants do not fight the eviction. Add one or two more months if they do. Using an expert lawyer will usually reduce the landlord's costs. However, trying it yourself or going through one or more nonspecialist lawyers usually results in starting the case over more than once. Delays and frustrations have their cost too. Legal fees start at several hundred dollars and can go over a thousand if the tenants choose to fight. Get an estimate from your lawyer in advance, and be sure you understand exactly how he or she charges. Most lawyers are honest: They want you to be happy with them when the case is over. So communicate thoroughly at the beginning.

The first question to ask your lawyer is: What are my chances of winning? If the chances are good, you may want to proceed. If the chances are slim, the results can be a catastrophe. Being sued by the tenants is a most unpleasant experience, even if you have insurance. Get an expert opinion before commencing your action.

Nonpayment, nuisance, and other breach-of-lease cases are usually quite winnable, at a reasonable cost, if the landlord has been responsible and done his or her job in the past. Naturally, in their defense, tenants may accuse the landlord of many things. But as long as their accusations are groundless, the tenants will not succeed.

Owner move-in cases, and other cases such as rehabilitation or renovation of a rental unit, in rent-control areas, are much more complex. If the landlord is acting truthfully and has complied with all of the rent board's technical requirements, he should succeed. Negotiating with the tenants in these situations, however, avoids the possibility of a long trial and thus usually reduces both parties' legal fees and the landlord's risk of failure.

How can these situations be avoided? Nonpayment-of-rent cases can be prevented by the landlord's thorough credit checks and employment verifications, plus the requirement of an adequate security deposit. The same is often true with nuisance cases. Most responsible, hard-working people do not stay up all night partying. A wise landlord does not accept the first tenant willing to pay a high rent. Future problems can be prevented by picking tenants who seem trustworthy, even if accepting them means reducing the rent.

Implementation and maintenance of a smooth owner-move-in eviction depends on the development of good relations with one's tenants. If the landlord-tenant relationship is one of mutual trust, requesting a tenant to move so that the owner or owner's relative can move in will not create suspicion. If tenants have had to hound the landlord for services, e.g., necessary repairs, however, an owner move-in can easily be interpreted as retaliation on the part of the landlord. And, ironically, the tenants who give you the most trouble are the ones you should go out of your way to please. Even if they do not respect you for it, a judge or a jury will.

24

Correct
Service
of a Notice

A THREE DAY NOTICE TO PAY OR QUIT is served as a remedy for a tenant's nonpayment of rent. A Three Day Notice to Perform Covenant is meant to cure breaches of a rental agreement other than the duty to pay rent. A Thirty Day Notice is typically intended to terminate a month-to-month tenancy. Suitable forms are available from stationery stores, but care must be taken in filling them out and serving them. [See Appendix D for examples.]

A landlord who wants to receive his rent on time must know the rules for enforcing payment. The most common tool is to serve a Three Day Notice to Pay or Quit. This does not always mean that you will follow the notice with an eviction. That depends on what the tenant does. If further action is needed, the Three Day Notice to Pay or Quit becomes quite important.

The tenant's rent must be overdue before a landlord can legally serve the notice. If the rent due-date falls on a weekend or holiday, the rent is actually not due until the following workday and is not overdue until the day after that. The notice should clearly name all tenants, subtenants, and other known adult occupants. The exact address and the precise amount of rent owed should be set out. The preprinted language in the form tells the tenant that either the rent must be paid to the landlord within three days of the service of the notice or they must leave. Late charges, utility charges, and other claims must not be included, although these may legitimately be due. Even if a notice is served midway in the month, the full month's rent should be demanded. Do not prorate the rent. Credit should be given for any partial payments, but not for a security deposit or the last month's rent.

The Three Day Notice to Perform Covenant, demanding that a lease covenant be complied with, is prepared in almost the same way. However, the precise nature of the tenant's violation must be spelled out: Specify both the lease requirement that is in breach and the tenant's exact violation. Like a tenant in a nonpayment-of-rent situation, the tenant who is in breach of covenant is given an opportunity to cure the breach or move out. When the breach is incurable, such as an unauthorized sublease or conduct creating a nuisance, a Three Day Notice to Quit, giving no alternative to the tenant, should be served.

Fill out the Thirty Day Notice with the same care and attention to detail as the other notices. This notice is used to end a month-to-month tenancy and may be served at any point during the month. However, if the rent is due weekly, or if the rental agreement specifically provides for it, as little as seven days' notice may be given. Unless the lease term is for more than a thirty-day period, this notice is effective to terminate a tenancy without cause in most of California. This is true for all commercial tenancies, wherever located. But for a residential tenancy in a rent-controlled city, "just cause" must be stated and proven. Typically, local laws add on a number of other very technical requirements with which landlords must comply.

The service of the Three or Thirty Day Notice on tenants is a strict legal matter. Anyone over eighteen, including the landlord, can serve it, but care should be taken to make sure all known adult occupants are individually given a copy, whether a landlord considers them tenants or not. The best method is to put a copy in the hands of each person. This is known as "personal service." If an individual is not at home, try to find him or her at work. If the tenant is not available there, you can leave the notice with a responsible person at either the tenant's home or workplace, but also mail a copy to the tenant at his or her residence by regular first-class mail. Finally, if no one is available to accept the notice at either the residence or the workplace, you may tape a copy on the door to the apartment and mail a copy first-class.

This is proper "substituted service." The Thirty Day Notice may also be served by certified mail. There is some legal authority in California, however, for giving the tenants five extra days to comply with the notice if they are not served personally, thus extending from three days to eight days the tenant's right to cure the default.

When a Thirty Day Notice is served, rent may be accepted for the period right up to the last day of the tenancy. However, if a landlord has accepted a "last month's rent," as opposed to a "security deposit," according to the terms of the lease, this amount will be applied to the final month's tenancy. Accepting rent for another month or for a period beyond the termination date will defeat the notice and cancel the eviction procedure.

None of the notices discussed here should be served to retaliate against a tenant. California law allows tenants a substantial defense based on the concept of retaliation. Improper service of a notice and accepting rent after the date a tenancy was terminated are the two most common mistakes landlords make when initiating an Unlawful Detainer action.

If litigation is necessary, there may be additional circumstances that require the reservice of one of these notices. Attorneys know that a mistake at this point can defeat the entire litigation. But in most cases, adherence to the rules will produce a proper notice that will have the desired effect. This is a skill landlords must learn in order to properly and economically manage rental property.

25 *Delaying Tactics*

WHEN AN INCOME PROPERTY OWNER needs to evict a tenant, he or she must use the legal system. No "self-help" is allowed, unless the property is a tourist hotel. Naturally, tenants have a right to contest a lawsuit, and often do, not necessarily in the hope of winning, but simply to "buy time." If the landlord cannot eventually collect a judgment, such as when the tenant is unemployed or has no assets, the tenant generally has nothing to lose and everything to gain by delaying the trial.

Although the time frame of an eviction proceeding is much shorter than other lawsuits (for example, a five-day rather than the typical thirty-day summons period), all the procedures of general litigation are available. After the owner's complaint, called an Unlawful

Detainer, is filed and served on the defendants, a variety of maneuvers are available to tenants who wish to challenge the landlord's case. In many cities, the necessary forms, or legal advice, are available free at convenient locations.

Common Delaying Tactics

Tenants can serve the landlord a "Motion to Quash," a claim that the lawsuit was not properly served on the defendants. Although the claim is usually without merit, its legitimacy must be decided by a judge. Some attorneys bring an extra copy of the complaint papers on the day of the hearing to serve the defendants again before entering the courtroom. The irony is, if the defendants lose the motion, they now have five days to file an answer. If they win the motion, but have just been served again, they also have five days to answer. What is the purpose? As stated above: to delay the lawsuit.

Tenants can use other pretrial motions that accuse the landlord of failing to "dot the i's" or "cross the t's" in his or her court papers. One such motion is called a "Demurrer"; another, a "Motion to Strike." Due to the technical nature of Unlawful Detainer lawsuits, a landlord will occasionally be required to make changes to the complaint and then re-serve the defendant. Use of an experienced landlord-tenant attorney from start to finish can minimize these risks. But because the tenant can employ the proceedings described above, win or lose, such tactics will delay the trial three or four weeks.

In addition to the above motions, there is also a procedure known as "Claim of Right to Possession": A "stranger" claims he is a subtenant and thus is entitled like the other defendants to his day in court. If he can prove his claim, even though the landlord had no knowledge of and did not permit the subtenancy, the "stranger" may be entitled to join the case and present new defenses and new delaying tactics.

Ultimately there will, however, be a trial. (By now the courtroom may begin to seem like home.) Assuming that the landlord/plaintiff is adequately prepared and that the merits of the case are strong, the owner should prevail. Sometimes the tenants fail to appear in court. Why? Often because they have achieved their purpose: months of free rent. At this point a landlord may wish he had paid the tenants to move out, just to avoid the frustration of the many delays. Indeed, early settlement is often recommended in eviction cases. It is often faster and less expensive than litigating the case through trial.

How can a landlord avoid such messy situations? Whatever the nature of the case—nonpayment of rent, nuisance, or owner move-in—all have both strengths and weaknesses. The landlord, with the help of a qualified professional, must carefully evaluate these aspects and the time and money that are inevitably involved in litigation. It is certainly better to know the many disadvantages in advance rather than embark on an expensive and risky venture. A simple settlement may be the logical and most attractive solution. A procedure known as a Stipulated Judgment may give both sides what they need. If done in a friendly manner, it will leave a better memory than "no-holds-barred" litigation.

26 *Enforcing the Judgment*

JUDGMENTS IN UNLAWFUL DETAINER cases are usually for possession of the premises and for money owed. This money typically represents unpaid rents plus court costs and sometimes attorney's fees. However, only a sheriff or a marshall can enforce an Unlawful Detainer judgment. No self-help is allowed.

If the case is won by default, it may proceed in two stages. First, because it can be done fairly quickly, and because the landlord is losing money every day, a Clerk's Judgment for Possession should be obtained. After this is completed and the landlord's losses have been cut, he can return to the court within six months for a money judgment.

To enforce a judgment for the return of a rental unit—whether obtained by default, at trial, or by stipulation—the landlord obtains a Writ of Execution from the court and proceeds to the sheriff. After a few days, the sheriff's office will post a five-day eviction notice at the rental property and then call the landlord to schedule the physical eviction. The landlord must meet the deputy at the rental property at the time of the eviction and be prepared to change the locks. If the tenants try to take possession of the property after the sheriff leaves, they are subject to arrest.

Often tenants move voluntarily shortly before the sheriff returns to enforce the eviction notice, although in some cases a "stranger" may remain at the property and try to delay the eviction by filing a claim with the court. This tactic is rarely successful. Tenants may also attempt to delay eviction by asking the court for "relief from forfeiture," claiming hardship. To win such a petition, tenants must pay all money owed to the landlord. A more common delay results when a tenant seeks a temporary stay of execution on the payment of some rent. Courts usually grant these requests for one to two weeks.

Appeals of Unlawful Detainer judgments are rare. When they are made, eviction will proceed, unless there is a special court order preventing eviction.

If tenants leave personal possessions behind after they have been evicted, they have fifteen days to return and recover abandoned items. If tenants leave by means other than eviction, a landlord must mail a Notice of Abandonment listing any belongings and notifying tenants that they have eighteen days to recover any possessions.

Collecting the Money Judgment

The easiest way for a landlord to collect the monetary portion of the judgment is to attach a tenant's bank account or garnish wages. To do this, a landlord must obtain a Writ of Execution from the clerk of the court and deliver it to the Sheriff's Department, where there is another form to fill out, and another filing fee. Keep photocopies of the tenant's rent checks in your file, and update the file once a year. This will provide all the information the sheriff needs. Note: You cannot garnish a welfare, social security, unemployment, pension, or disability check, or most federal paychecks.

Although the security deposit must be credited against the amount collected, a landlord can deduct the cost of repairs for damages beyond normal wear and tear, and other legitimate expenses, from the security deposit.

If you do not know where the tenant has gone, examine the rental application: Calling the job or personal references may provide clues. Otherwise, go to the Post Office. Often a person will notify the Postal Service of the new address. Try the telephone directory, too. Call the telephone information number and ask if there is a new listing. That number can provide the address through a reverse directory which is available in some libraries.

If these attempts prove unsuccessful, you may want to hand the judgment over to a collection agency for the usual 50 percent fee on whatever they collect. Your attorney may also be interested in such a proposal. Collection agencies have access to computer data banks that may tell them—even years later—where your former tenants now work or have opened a bank account. You usually need the tenant's social security number to do this, however.

A former tenant can also be brought back to court for what is called a "judgment debtor's examination." He must first be personally served with an Order of Examination. If you are able to locate him, have him properly served. If he shows up, inquire where he works and about all other relevant financial matters.

If you are successful in having the judgment paid off, you must then file an "Acknowledgment of Satisfaction" with the court. This is public evidence that the tenant has paid off the debt. If he or she tries to get a real estate loan, the bank may require this. In fact, this situation sometimes results in an odd phenomenon. Years after you have given up on collecting the judgment, the tenant may send you a cashier's check and an Acknowledgment of Satisfaction form to sign for this very reason.

In view of the potential obstacles, try to evaluate the collectibility of a money judgment before going to court. A landlord has little choice about seeking an eviction if the rent is not being paid. Beyond that, many wise and experienced income property owners assume that they never will be paid the delinquent rent. This is usually a safe assumption, though probably the most valuable resource a landlord can have in this situation is a verified rental application that provides clues for collection.

1933

Litigation Happens

*"All virtue is summed up
in dealing justly."*

—**Aristotle**, ca. 325 BCE
Nicomachean Ethics

27 *Small Claims Court*

S MALL CLAIMS COURT IS ACTUALLY a division of a city's Municipal Court. Though it is open to anyone, there are limits to the ways a landlord can use this court. Generally, a landlord's claim should be based on a month-to-month tenancy for nonpayment of rent with a maximum amount of $5,000. If possession of the premises is in dispute, the claim should be brought in the regular Municipal Court.

Tenants sometimes use Small Claims Court to sue a landlord for the return of a security deposit or an illegal "finder's fee." In these cases, sometimes the court awards the tenant "punitive damages." The court also has jurisdiction to order a landlord to make necessary repairs, and it can even be used for a small personal injury case.

For income property owners, the main advantages of Small Claims Court are the inexpensive filing fee and the fact that the clerk of the court provides a complaint form. You do not need an attorney. In fact, attorneys are not allowed. Small Claims Court might be an appropriate place for a landlord to bring a suit when possession of the rental unit is no longer an issue. If a tenant breaches a lease by moving out early and the landlord must find a new tenant, for instance, this may be the best court in which to bring a claim for any lost rent.

It may also be a good place to sue a tenant for damages to rental property that exceed the amount of the tenant's security deposit. Before suing, a written account of the landlord's use of the security deposit, including a list of the repair costs, should be sent to the tenant. If a landlord intentionally and in "bad faith" does not return the correct amount of security deposit within 21 days, "punitive damages" of $600—in excess of the actual amount to which the tenant would be entitled—can be awarded.

The disadvantages of using Small Claims Court include the $5,000 limit on claims, the delays encountered, and the restriction from using lawyers. A case can take several months to get to trial, and if the defendant loses, he or she can appeal the case to Superior Court for a new trial. When a defendant appeals, the sheriff cannot enforce the Small Claims Court judgment in the meantime. Another disadvantage of using this court is that it is easy for defendants to contest. They do not need to file a written response; they do not need to hire a lawyer. They need only show up in court. (Cases heard in Municipal Court require a written answer which usually requires an attorney to prepare.)

The procedures of a trial in Small Claims Court are informal. But it is important that the action be brought to trial as soon as possible after the claim arises. That way the documentary evidence and the testimony are fresh.

The plaintiff (and the defendant) should organize the evidence carefully. Explain your case clearly. Judges usually prefer a chronological explanation. If English is not your primary language, a friend or relative can interpret. Do not interrupt your adversary's presentation. Wait patiently. Then ask the judge if you may respond. Your patience and reasonableness can only help your case, whereas emotionalism and displays of anger will not. Don't ramble on. You may present photographs or ask questions of the other party, but never argue.

There is no appeal if the landlord-plaintiff (the one who initiates an action) loses. On the other hand, if the defendant loses, he or she can appeal the case to the Superior Court. If that happens, the owner may need an attorney. At this point the landlord should notify the insurance company, if he or she has not already done so. (Note once again how important it is that landlords have the correct type of liability insurance for their income property. Their homeowner's policy is not enough. In addition to standard premises liability, they should have "wrongful eviction" coverage. Landlords should consult their insurance company or broker for this type of information.)

In conclusion, the limitations in Small Claims Court may outweigh what one saves by bringing a case to trial. On the other hand, the advantages of having a professional present the case in Municipal Court must be balanced against the attorney's fees saved by going it alone in Small Claims Court.

28

Personal Injury Cases

O F ALL THE UNPLEASANT SITUATIONS in which an income property owner can find himself or herself, being sued by a tenant tops the list. Tenants' attorneys usually prosecute these cases on a contingency basis—i.e., their fee is a percentage of the amount recovered. Thus, as long as the lawyer thinks it's a worthy case, the cost of bringing the action is usually not an obstacle, even for an impoverished renter. Typical suits are breach of the landlord's duty to provide habitable premises, personal injury suffered on the premises, wrongful eviction, and harassment. An additional allegation of emotional distress often increases the overall size of the damage claim.

In the past, tenants assumed all the risks when living in rental property. A landlord's only duty was to provide the land on which a structure existed or on which a lessee might build. But as landlord-tenant law evolved over the centuries, the legal relationship between landlord and tenant, particularly in urban residential housing, evolved as well.

These days it is common for a tenant to file a suit claiming that the owner neglected to perform certain duties and that neglect has somehow damaged the plaintiff. A defect in the building, such as a broken stairwell handrail, or a general failure to provide habitable premises, are examples of such neglect. If the tenant or a guest is injured or becomes ill as a result, a claim for the personal injury is legitimate.

Recent developments now allow mental suffering, whether accompanied by physical suffering or not, to also be the subject of a court's award of damages. Typical sources of these judgments are: invasion of privacy or, in a rent-controlled jurisdiction, wrongful eviction. If a nuisance condition, such as drug dealing, exists in the building, the tenants and even the occupants of neighboring buildings can bring suit. Any lease provision intended to absolve the landlord of such possibilities is unenforceable.

The most recent development to increase an owner's exposure to litigation is liability for lack of security. Even when a criminal attack is the actual cause of injury, such as a rape, under certain circumstances, the landlord will be held legally responsible. If security to the building was below the legal standard—even though the failure is a very minor thing, such as forgetting to change a light bulb in a garage—it can result in a negligence claim. And if a landlord advertises the enhanced "security" of an apartment, the risk of getting sued by a crime victim in the building becomes that much greater. Professional property management companies can be named in the lawsuit as well, although quite often they have a clause in their contract requiring the building owner to indemnify them, i.e., pay their defense costs and any damages awarded to the plaintiff.

A landlord is usually not responsible for fire damage unless it is caused by his or her negligence. But if smoke detectors are not installed or maintained in all areas requiring them, the owner will be liable.

Another theory of liability developed by the courts is one known as "strict liability." Based on the law's concern for the public's well-being, courts hold manufacturers liable for any defect in their products— even if the manufacturer had not been negligent. At one time, this concept was also applied to rental property owners. The most famous case involved a tenant who was injured by broken glass in her shower door. If it had been safety glass, it would not have broken. The current owner of the building at the time of the accident, who was neither the builder nor the original owner, had to pay for the damages though he had no previous knowledge of the dangerous condition. The Court of Appeal put the burden of safety, to find "strict liability," on the landlord as a practical means to try to ensure safe housing. Thus, income property owners became responsible, without actual negligence, for latent defects on their property. More recently, however, the California Supreme Court rejected the concept of "strict liability" as applied to landlords.

On the opposite end of the spectrum of situations involving actual or ethical responsibility are intentional acts committed by the owner. Many landlords have no doubt experienced an impulse to harm an onerous tenant at one time or another—and the feeling was probably mutual. If a landlord acts on such an impulse, however, a judge or a jury can and will award punitive damages—an amount in addition to actual damages—to the plaintiff as a means to punish the guilty party. An eviction based on a false claim, or any other reckless action which harms someone, can be the basis for such an award. An insurance company cannot and will not pay a penalty of punitive damages. The moneys will come out of the owner's pocket, and may even result in the sheriff seizing and selling the rental property to raise the necessary funds.

Using common sense and courtesy in dealing with tenants and making a diligent effort to repair property defects promptly will minimize a landlord's chances of being sued. Never ignore tenants' requests for repairs. Owners should document all complaints and requests, including their own response. Routinely check the premises for conditions that may not be easily noticed. Insurance companies will sometimes help with the inspection and even provide an expert. After all, they, too, want to avoid suits. To minimize the personal and financial stress created by litigation, every income property owner should obtain adequate insurance. If you rent out a house in which you used to live, the standard policy often needs to be enhanced. Get to know your insurance agent. Let him or her know, in writing, that you need adequate protection from potential suits by your tenants. Given the well-known protenant bias that juries in some urban areas exhibit when deciding claims brought against a landlord, high limits in the insurance coverage should be specified. Some policies do not cover things such as slander and wrongful eviction. Make sure your insurance does.

29

Understanding Legal Aid

S O FAR IN THIS BOOK we have examined many situations in which a landlord's compassion and respect for tenants is the most effective factor in avoiding or minimizing stressful and costly legal disputes. As effective as these approaches are, however, extremely difficult landlord-tenant disputes periodically arise. In these problematic situations, landlords must seek relief in the court system, which often means lost rent, time-consuming legal proceedings, and expensive legal fees. Ironically, tenants with the least financial resources may be able to obtain expert legal representation for free. Since this fact is common knowledge to many low-income tenants, they naturally look into the availability of such services when sued by a landlord. They can find legal assistance by calling their local rent board or bar association for appropriate referrals.

There are three basic sources of free, or almost free, legal representation available to tenants:

1. **Legal Aid Offices.** Most counties have some type of legal aid office funded by the federal Legal Services Corporation. These offices usually have some members of their staff specifically devoted to helping tenants. They are extremely well-versed in the law and are vigilant advocates for their clients.

2. **Private Attorneys.** Representation can also be obtained from a private attorney or law firm that accepts referrals from the bar association on a "pro bono publica" (for the good of the people) basis. Although these attorneys are not always knowledgeable about landlord-tenant law, they may be quite experienced in general litigation. They can also consult with experts as needed.

3. **Self-Representation.** Tenants can also represent themselves "in propria persona," as their own attorney. Typically, a local legal clinic or tenants' organization provides them with printed forms and excellent advice. Although they may appear alone in court, their legal briefs usually assert their position quite effectively.

Legal assistance for the tenant can often result in instant defeat for the landlord. The field of landlord-tenant law is so technical that a seemingly trivial mistake can be fatal to the landlord's case. The tenant's representative will comb through the landlord's lawsuit searching for just such defects. The suit may be dismissed immediately, and, adding insult to injury, the landlord can be served with a bill for the tenant's attorney's fees and court costs.

Should the landlord's case survive the initial "technical" challenges raised by the tenant, the case may yet be complicated by the tenant's use of numerous "substantive" defenses, such as habitability defects and improper rent increases. The legal process may require several court appearances in addition to depositions, answering interrogatories, and other tedious tasks, before the case finally goes to trial. Meanwhile, rent continues to go uncollected, and the certainty of a successful conclusion can seem to slip away.

The delays incurred can take two or three months, or even longer. Furthermore, if an action is mishandled or if extraordinary difficulties arise, the case may ultimately involve six months or a year of litigation. Of course, this situation seems unfair to the owner since he or she is losing rent and paying attorney's fees while it is costing the tenant nothing. Even the landlord's use of an attorney may not avoid this common scenario.

Since the tenant's advocate is often an expert in defeating landlords, I advise owners to find not just an experienced attorney, but a *landlord-tenant specialist*. These attorneys can very quickly analyze the situation and suggest an appropriate course of action, which may well include negotiating a settlement of the case without further delay or the cost of continued litigation.

Attorneys are trained to be objective and unemotional. Their role is to provide the most efficient method to solve a problem and preserve their client's investment. Their advice may at times be somewhat bitter medicine. But even if it includes waiving the rent and allowing a tenant an extended move-out date, the alternatives would probably be even more expensive and frustrating.

Is this a fair situation? From the landlord's perspective, no. But it represents a balancing of interests between the income-property owner and the presumably rent-paying tenant. Though the balance may seem to tip strongly in the tenant's favor, a landlord's best protection is simply to screen potential tenants carefully and thus avoid those whose employment and credit histories indicate a problem.

30

The Attorney's Role

AS EARLY AS THE TIME OF SHAKESPEARE, and no doubt before, people have expressed their distrust of lawyers. And for centuries to come, people will probably continue to have some discomfort with the legal profession. But in a civilized society, a nonviolent solution to conflict must be achieved. Lawyers, as representatives of disagreeing parties, enter the fray to try to achieve fair and just resolutions in legal disputes. They offer this valuable service for a price, but they are not always needed. A wise user of legal services knows when representation is necessary and when it is a superfluous luxury.

There are many legal circumstances in which a lawyer need not be involved. If you are preparing a rental agreement, there are suitable forms and even software programs available that a landlord can adapt to fit his or her particular situation, although for radical changes, a professional is recommended. At rent board hearings, an individual is permitted to have an attorney, but it may not be necessary: Apartment managers or management companies can often do the job as well. If you sue or are sued in Small Claims Court, no lawyers are allowed. However, if you have to argue the case again on appeal in Superior Court, you may want and are permitted to use an attorney there.

There are many situations in which a landlord *should* use a lawyer. Consider, for example, a situation in which a landlord has no choice but to evict a tenant because he is not paying the rent. In rent-controlled cities, the landlord would need a lawyer to evict the tenant. If a landlord starts such a case without a lawyer, he may have to obtain one later if the case becomes difficult. Landlords sometimes file Unlawful Detainer actions on their own, but if the tenant contests it, an attorney will almost definitely be needed for the trial. The landlord should at least seek a consultation. If a tenant sues a landlord, the need for a lawyer's services becomes even more urgent. Remember: Professionals, even experts, need time to prepare. Hiring a lawyer should therefore be done well in advance of the actual trial.

Leases sometimes have an attorney's fee clause. Nevertheless, there is no guarantee that the court will award them to the landlord, nor is there any certainty that a landlord can collect them from the other party involved. And reliance on such a clause does not release the landlord from his duty to pay his attorney's bill. If you lose a case, you may also have to pay the other side's attorney's fees.

There are specific situations in which a landlord *should* definitely consider using an attorney. If a tenant is represented by an attorney or if a tenant files some type of technical motion, such as a "demurrer," against you in court, you will need legal counsel. The strategy of tenants or their attorney is sometimes just a delaying tactic. Strange and complex arguments in a demurrer, for instance, delay the ultimate trial. If a tenant demands a jury trial, the landlord definitely needs an experienced lawyer. If a tenant claims the landlord has violated a local rent ordinance, or is discriminating or retaliating against him, an attorney's expertise is often vital to the landlord's case.

Deciding to retain a legal professional's services is the first step; finding the right lawyer is next. Cost is always a consideration and attorneys' fees vary. There are lawyers who specialize in a given field such as landlord-tenant law, who do a very competent job and who charge fairly. If you do not know of one, ask a friend. Selecting one at random is risky. Local apartment house owners' associations usually list several. Also, do not expect a flat fee. Most attorneys, particularly those specializing, realize how unpredictable any case can be. They want to neither overcharge nor undercharge you.

They simply want to be paid for the time they spend on the case, time, by the way, that includes speaking on the telephone. Surprisingly, hiring an expert often saves both time and money because of the knowledge of particular techniques which makes an attorney a specialist in a certain field.

Try to get referrals to several qualified specialists—you can compare their rates, their expertise, and your general impressions. Then make a decision. The Yellow Pages are a good source for locating attorneys with expertise in fields such as landlord-tenant law. But be aware: An attorney's self-promotion in an advertisement is no guarantee. Individual attorneys will have varying perceptions of the experience necessary to qualify as an "expert." The person who does the hiring must make the final judgment-call.

Many lawyers charge only a small fee for a short consultation, from $50 to $100. At that time, they may also be able to give you an estimate of their overall fees to handle a case as well as the necessary court costs. Be prepared to sign a written fee agreement. This contract should make all the terms and policies very clear. Lawyers typically have high office overhead, so their hourly rates may vary from $150 to $200 per hour or more.

A person should decide whether to use a lawyer in the same way they decide whether to obtain other services. Is hiring an attorney worth the cost? How much do they stand to lose if they don't hire one? Even without a lawsuit pending, an attorney can be an effective negotiator in a dispute. Sometimes even a single letter from an attorney can resolve a troublesome situation. If that does not work, the lawyer should be able to advise you whether proceeding to court is a good idea, or whether it is wiser to drop the whole matter. A lawyer can be consulted about almost any kind of landlord-tenant dispute and can probably provide a short but effective education in the course of one brief meeting. That way, a small problem can be solved before it becomes big. Indeed, the *Code of Hammurabi*, which is mankind's earliest known written set of laws, prescribes that:

> *All parties take reasonable steps to resolve*
> *disputes at the lowest level of litigation.*

Everyone can benefit by heeding the advice of this basic tenet.

Dear Landlord

by Bob Dylan

Dear landlord,
Please don't put a price on my soul.
My burden is heavy,
My dreams are beyond control.
When that steamboat whistle blows,
I'm gonna give you all I got to give,
And I do hope you receive it well,
Dependin' on the way you feel that you live.

Dear landlord,
Please heed these words that I speak.
I know you've suffered much,
But in this you are not so unique.
All of us, at times, we might work too hard
To have it too fast and too much,
And anyone can fill his life up
With things he can see but he just cannot touch.

Dear landlord,
Please don't dismiss my case.
I'm not about to argue,
I'm not about to move to no other place.
Now, each of us has his own special gift
And you know this was meant to be true,
And if you don't underestimate me,
I won't underestimate you.

A Rent Control Ordinances

BERKELEY

Berkeley has one of the strictest local rent and eviction ordinances in California. It allows eviction only for very limited purposes. Rents are strictly regulated. Vacant apartments are to be rented at a reduced amount. This provision is being phased out under a state law which supersedes it (Civil Code Section 1954.53). All rental units must be registered.

Units constructed after June 3, 1980, and owner-occupied single-family residences and duplexes are exempt from this rent control ordinance. Violations are subject to criminal and civil penalties. Interest must be paid on security deposits.

Copies of this law can be obtained from:

BERKELEY RENT STABILIZATION BOARD
2125 Milvia Street
Berkeley, CA 94704
Tel: (510) 644-6128

BEVERLY HILLS

Beverly Hills has a moderate form of rent control. It allows annual increases of 8 percent (10 percent for luxury units) or the Consumer Price Index percentage, whichever is less. "Capital expenditure surcharges" are also allowed, as well as additional increases for utility expenses. Extra adult occupants can be charged 10 percent more. Condominiums and units built after October 20, 1978, are exempt, as also are some luxury units.

After a unit becomes vacant, the owner may charge whatever the market will bear (vacancy decontrol). Just cause, e.g., nonpayment of rent, owner move-in, etc., must be proven to evict. Penalties for violations include criminal as well as civil, i.e., lawsuits by the tenant.

To obtain a copy of this ordinance contact:

BEVERLY HILLS ADJUSTMENT BOARD
455 N. Rexford
Beverly Hills, CA 90210
Tel: (310) 285-1031

CAMPBELL

Campbell has a very mild ordinance. Single-family homes and duplexes are exempt. There is no formula for rent control, except that the increases be "reasonable." After a unit becomes vacant, whatever the market bears can be charged (vacancy decontrol). No restrictions on evictions.

Copies of this law can be obtained from:

CAMPBELL RENT MEDIATION PROGRAM
1245 S. Wincester Blvd., Suite 200
San Jose, CA 95128
Tel: (408) 243-8365

COTATI

Rather significant rent control restrictions are mandated by Cotati's local law. Annual increases of only 66 percent of the rise in the Consumer Price Index are allowed. Vacancy control existed until recently, limiting what rent could be charged a new tenant after the unit was vacant. However, this is being phased out by a superseding state law (Civil Code Section 1954.53). Vacancies will be totally decontrolled after January 1, 1999.

Evictions are limited to certain typical forms of just cause. Newer buildings (those built after September 23, 1980) and buildings with three units or less, when owner-occupied, are exempt. All other units must be registered.

Obtain a copy of this ordinance by contacting:

COTATI RENT APPEAL BOARD
201 W. Sierra
Cotati, CA 94931
Tel: (707) 792-4600

EAST PALO ALTO

East Palo Alto has a strict type of rent control law. All units must be registered. The landlord may raise rent, but the tenant may petition the Rent Board. The board decides on the allowable annual adjustments. Evictions are limited to a typical few just causes. Owners of four or fewer units are exempt. Vacancy control prevailed until recently, disallowing increases to the market rate on vacant units. But state law has now superseded that, phasing in complete vacancy decontrol by January 1, 1999. Violations are subject to criminal and civil penalties.

For more information, contact:

EAST PALO ALTO RENT STABILIZATION BOARD
2415 University Avenue
East Palo Alto, CA 94303
Tel: (650) 853-3100

HAYWARD

Hayward has a mild form of rent control; this ordinance allows 5 percent annual increases, plus increased utility costs if documented. Just cause is required to evict. Violations are subject to minor penalties. Vacancies result in decontrol, allowing market rent, so long as the owner spends $200 on improvements. Newer units (those built after July 1, 1979) are completely exempt, as are dwellings owned by someone owning four or less units. Interest is required on security deposits.

Copies of this ordinance can be obtained from:

HAYWARD RENT REVIEW BOARD
25151 Clawiter Road
Hayward, CA 94545-2731
Tel: (510) 293-5540

LOS ANGELES

Rent increases of 3 percent to 8 percent each year are allowed in the City of Los Angeles, depending on the Consumer Price Index. Higher increases are obtained by petition. Consequently, this is a less restrictive law compared to some communities. However, registration of all units is required, and just cause must be proven for eviction. Luxury units, newer units (those built after October

1, 1978), and renovated units are exempt, as are single-family homes.

Rent can be raised to the market value after a vacancy. Penalties include triple damages plus attorney fees. Interest on security deposits is required although this has been appealed in a court challenge.

To obtain a copy of this law, or more information, contact:

> **LOS ANGELES RENT ADJUSTMENT COMMISSION**
> 400 South Main, 6th Floor
> Los Angeles, CA 90013
> Tel: (213) 847-7368

LOS GATOS

A moderate type of control ordinance, the Los Gatos law allows annual rent increases of up to 5 percent, depending on the local Consumer Price Index. But market rent can be charged a new tenant after the unit becomes vacant. Single-family homes and condominiums are exempt. Registration is not required. No just cause need be present to support an eviction.

A copy of the ordinance is available at:

> **LOS GATOS RENT MEDIATION**
> 1245 S. Wincester Blvd., Suite 200
> San Jose, CA 95128
> Tel: (408) 243-8565

OAKLAND

Oakland has a mild ordinance. Increases of up to 6 percent are allowed, 12 percent after a vacancy. Newer units (those constructed after January 1, 1983) and substantially rehabilitated ones are exempt. No registration is required. No just cause for eviction is required. Only repeat violations are seriously penalized.

Copies of this ordinance can be obtained from:

OAKLAND RESIDENTIAL RENT ARBITRATION BOARD
1333 Broadway, Fourth Floor
Oakland, CA 94612
Tel: (510) 238-3721

PALM SPRINGS

Palm Springs has a relatively strict ordinance. Just cause for evictions is required. Civil penalties, including attorney's fees, are awarded for violations. However, rent controls are removed after a tenant voluntarily vacates. Registration is required. Newer units (after April 1, 1979) and buildings of four units or fewer, if owner-occupied, are exempt. The rent increase formula is 75 percent of the annual Consumer Price Index, but a landlord may petition for further increases based on "hardship."

Obtain a copy of this law by contacting:

PALM SPRINGS RENT REVIEW COMMISSION
3200 E. Tahquitz Canyon Way
Palm Springs, CA 92262
Tel: (619) 778-8465

SAN FRANCISCO

San Francisco has a moderate form of rent and eviction control. The rent may increase at 60 percent of the Consumer Price Index, but not more than 7 percent in any twelve-month period. Just cause of the usual type (e.g., owner move-in, nuisance, nonpayment of rent) is required for eviction. Special language on the Notices to Quit is required, plus copies of all notices (except for nonpayment of rent) must be filed at the Rent Board. No registration is required, and the landlord may charge any rent after a tenant vacates or is evicted. However, the rent is controlled again for the new tenant. Newer units (those built after June 1979) and "substantially rehabilitated" buildings over 50 years old (with some very strict procedures) are exempt.

Individual petitions to the Rent Board may result in special increases (or decreases) based on increased costs, such as capital improvement costs. A hearing officer may consider a variety of factors including maintenance expenses, rent-increase history, and failures to make repairs. Tenants may contest claims by the landlord, and can request rent reduction as a result of an owner's negligence.

Violations usually result in the landlord being sued by very seasoned tenant attorneys. Judgments of hundreds of thousands of dollars, especially for fraudulent owner-move-in cases, are not uncommon. Criminal prosecution almost never occurs.

To obtain a copy, contact:

RENT STABILIZATION AND ARBITRATION BOARD
25 Van Ness Avenue, Suite 320
San Francisco, CA 94102
Tel: (415) 252-4600 or (415) 252-4660

SAN JOSE

San Jose's ordinance is weak because there is no need to show just cause for eviction and the allowable rent increases are generous. Increases greater than 8 percent per year are subject to mediation and arbitration if the tenant seeks it. Registration of units is required, but single units and duplexes are exempt, as are units constructed after September 7, 1979.

For a copy of this ordinance, write to:

SAN JOSE ADVISORY COMMITTEE ON RENTS
4 N. Second Street, Suite 600
San Jose, CA 95113-1305
Tel: (408) 277-5431

SANTA MONICA

Santa Monica's ordinance has been one of the strictest in the state since 1979. It has also been the subject of a great deal of litigation. Just cause for eviction is required and criminal penalties for violations are possible; however, tenant suits against landlords are the more common event. The vacancy control provision, preventing rent increases to the market rate after a tenant moves out, is being phased out pursuant to a recently passed state law.

One fairly unique provision is that landlords must place security deposits in interest-bearing accounts. Also, rent increases cannot be made if there are any housing, health, or safety code violations. Registration of the unit is required. Rent increases are quite modest and are decided annually by the Rent Control Board, but individual landlord petitions for increased expenses will be considered.

Owner-occupied buildings of three or fewer units are exempt, as are buildings constructed after April 10, 1979.

For more information or for a copy of this local law, contact:

> **SANTA MONICA RENT CONTROL BOARD**
> 1685 Main Street, Room 202
> Santa Monica, CA 90401
> Tel: (310) 458-8751

THOUSAND OAKS

Thousand Oaks has a moderately strict local ordinance. It has rigid control on annual rent increases, between 3 percent to 7 percent. The increase allowed is 75 percent of the Consumer Price Index, but the rent may be brought to market value after a tenant moves. Just cause is required for eviction. There are no criminal penalties, but the tenant may sue in a civil court and be awarded attorney fees. Registration of units is mandated. Exceptions to this rent formula are "luxury" units, buildings of four units or fewer, and units constructed after June 30, 1980.

One unique feature is an exemption allowable if senior citizens are provided with long-term leases. Also, individual landlord petitions for a reasonable return on capital improvements will be considered.

Copies of this ordinance can be obtained from:

> **RENT ADJUSTMENT COMMISSION**
> 2100 Thousand Oaks Boulevard
> Thousand Oaks, CA 91362
> Tel: (805) 449-2100

WEST HOLLYWOOD

West Hollywood is a strict eviction and rent-control city. However, the toughest provision for landlords—vacancy control (keeping units below market value after vacancy)—is being phased out because of a recently passed state law.

Annual rent increases are set by the Rent Stabilization Committee, but they are limited to 75 percent of the Consumer Price Index. Individual landlord petitions for increased maintenance or capital improvements are considered.

Registration of units, just cause for evictions, and interest on security deposits are all required. Units built after July 1, 1979, are exempt from rent controls, but not eviction controls. Tenants may bring suit for landlord violations. They can be awarded all their attorney fees plus damages of three times their actual loss.

To obtain a copy of this law, contact:

RENT STABILIZATION COMMISSION
8300 Santa Monica Boulevard
West Hollywood, CA 90069
Tel: (213) 848-6450

B

Where to Obtain Standard Rental Forms

The California Apartment Association (CAA) serves rental property owners and managers throughout California. It is the largest statewide rental housing trade association in the country. CAA represents over 25,000 rental housing owners and professionals who represent more than 1.5 million rental units. It is comprised of 22 local-member apartment associations throughout the state. In order to obtain standard rental agreement forms, contact your local apartment association, which you will find listed below.

CAA also distributes 60 other forms for use in the rental housing industry. CAA-approved forms have been reviewed for legality and are updated every year. There is a form for nearly every transaction and situation in the rental housing industry.

If you would like more information about the forms and services that CAA provides, contact either the CAA Headquarters in Sacramento or any of the following local associations.

CALIFORNIA APARTMENT ASSOCIATION HEADQUARTERS
980 Ninth Street, Suite 2150
Sacramento, CA 95814-2741
Tel: (916) 447-7881 • FAX: (916) 447-7903

Local Member Associations

ACTION APARTMENT ASSOCIATION
2812 Santa Monica Blvd., Suite 203
Santa Monica, CA 90404
(310) 828-7628

APARTMENT ASSOCIATION OF GREATER FRESNO
PO Box 26778
Fresno, CA 93729-6778
(209) 252-5125

APARTMENT ASSOCIATION OF GREATER INLAND EMPIRE
9227 Haven Ave., Suite 250
Rancho Cucamonga, CA 91730
(909) 949-0711

APARTMENT ASSOCIATION OF MONTEREY COUNTY
975 Cass Street
Monterey, CA 93940
(408) 649-4704

APARTMENT ASSOCIATION OF ORANGE COUNTY
12822 Garden Grove Blvd., Suite D
Garden Grove, CA 92643-2010
(714) 638-5550

BERKELEY PROPERTY OWNERS ASSOCIATION
2005 Hopkins Street
Berkeley, CA 94707
(510) 525-3666

CAA / SOUTHERN LOS ANGELES COUNTY CHAPTER
PO Box 3278
Long Beach, CA 90803-0278
(800) 305-7522

CENTRAL COAST RENTAL HOUSING ASSOCIATION
PO Box 101
Santa Maria, CA 93456
(805) 928-3988

MARIN INCOME PROPERTY ASSOCIATION
PO Box 150315
San Rafael, CA 94915
(415) 491-4461

NORTH COAST RENTAL HOUSING ASSOCIATION
PO Box 12172
Santa Rosa, CA 95406
(707) 526-9526

NORTH VALLEY PROPERTY OWNERS ASSOCIATION
813 East Fifth Avenue
Chico, CA 95926
(916) 345-1321

RENTAL HOUSING ASSOCIATION
Contra Costa–Solano–Napa Counties
1070 Concord Ave., Suite 120
Concord, CA 94520
(510) 686-3234 • (800) 600-8001

RENTAL HOUSING ASSOCIATION OF
NORTHERN ALAMEDA COUNTY
2201 Broadway, Suite 311
Oakland, CA 94612
(510) 893-9873

RENTAL HOUSING ASSOCIATION OF
SOUTHERN ALAMEDA COUNTY
1264 A Street
Hayward, CA 94541
(510) 537-0340

RENTAL PROPERTY ASSOCIATION OF CENTRAL CALIFORNIA
400 12th Street, Suite 14
Modesto, CA 95354
(209) 529-3055

RENTAL PROPERTY ASSOCIATION OF MERCED COUNTY
PO Box 2455
Merced, CA 95344
(209) 723-4797

SACRAMENTO VALLEY APARTMENT ASSOCIATION
221 Lathrop Way, Suite M
Sacramento, CA 95815
(916) 920-1120

SAN DIEGO COUNTY APARTMENT ASSOCIATION
2727 Camino del Rio South, Suite 327
San Diego, CA 92108
(619) 297-1000

SAN FRANCISCO APARTMENT ASSOCIATION
333 Hayes Street, Suite 100
San Francisco, CA 94102
(415) 255-2288

SAN JOAQUIN COUNTY RENTAL PROPERTY ASSOCIATION
840 N. El Dorado Street
Stockton, CA 95202
(209) 944-9266

SANTA BARBARA RENTAL PROPERTY ASSOCIATION
3887 State Street, Suite 7
Santa Barbara, CA 93105
(805) 687-7007

TRI-COUNTY APARTMENT ASSOCIATION
792 Meridian Way, Suite A
San Jose, CA 95126
(408) 297-0483

Sources of Insurance

As emphasized throughout this book, having the correct type of liability insurance on your income property is extremely important.

Make sure you have a comprehensive policy specifically designed for apartment houses and other tenant-occupied dwellings. Mere fire coverage is definitely not enough. A very broad, or "comprehensive," policy is designed for accidents caused by any type of negligence. No insurance policy will protect an owner from intentional wrongs such as assault and battery. However, a comprehensive policy should cover "wrongful eviction" and "attempted wrongful eviction" as well as the "emotional distress" and other claims that flow from them.

Some policies clearly state that "wrongful eviction" is covered. Some exclude it altogether, and a policyholder will not have coverage for such a claim. Also, certain properties, such as a single-family house with an illegal "in-law" unit, will not be covered under the typical homeowner's policy. Those policies usually do not cover any "business activity" conducted on the premises, such as an illegal rental unit.

It is always best to indicate clearly, in writing, to your insurance agent that you want coverage for any claim by a tenant, including "wrongful eviction."

The following companies have been offering the correct type of liability insurance to California landlords, and properly defending claims against them, for many years. Nevertheless, they have the right to change their policy and to exclude certain "perils" when writing a new policy. Just like earthquake coverage, wrongful eviction insurance is something to be sure you are obtaining or, if not, then at least be aware that you do not have it.

FARMERS INSURANCE GROUP: (415) 296-8282

FIREMAN'S FUND: (415) 777-3050

TRAVELERS: (415) 956-3990

(As of the date of this publication, Allstate and State Farm have left this market.)

All of the above companies have agents, sometimes many, in cities throughout the state. The quickest source for finding a local agent is the Yellow Pages of your telephone directory.

Ask the right questions, read the "liability coverage" and "personal injury" sections of the policy, and put your demands to your agent for this specific type of coverage in writing. If a claim arises later, you should then be covered. The insurance company will pay the defense cost for a law firm and, unless it appears clearly to be the result of an intentional wrong by the owner, they will pay the settlement or judgment as well.

D APPENDIX

Standard Legal Notices

The following four documents are the most common legal notices that a landlord would serve on his or her tenants. Although a landlord can serve these notices himself by filling in the blanks with the appropriate names, addresses, and amounts, I highly recommend retaining the services of an attorney who will do the job correctly.

Each notice includes the provisions of the rent-control ordinance of the City of San Francisco. Check for recent amendments, especially regarding owner move-in cases. If the premises in question are outside of that city, disregard the language that deals with the city's administrative code. Your local rent-control jurisdiction may require you to incorporate the provisions of your city into the body of the notice. Once again, the best advice is to consult an attorney who specializes in landlord-tenant litigation.

THREE DAY NOTICE TO PAY RENT OR QUIT

TO: _____and DOES I-X

<small>TENANT(S) IN POSSESSION</small>

YOU ARE HEREBY notified that the rent is now due and payable on the premises now held and occupied by you, being those premises situated in the City of _____, County of _____, commonly known as *(address or other identifying information)*_____

_____

Your account is delinquent in the amount of $_____, being the rent for the periods:

      FROM: TO: AMOUNT:

YOU ARE HEREBY required to pay said rent in full within three (3) days or to remove from and deliver up possession of the above-mentioned premises to *(specify person by name: e.g., landlord or landlord's agent)*_____, located at *(payment address)*_____, who is authorized to receive same, or legal proceedings will be instituted against you to recover possession of said premises, to declare the forfeiture of the lease or rental agreement under which you occupy said premises, and to recover rents and damages together with court costs and attorney's fees.

ADVICE REGARDING THIS NOTICE IS AVAILABLE FROM THE SAN FRANCISCO RENT STABILIZATION AND ARBITRATION BOARD. YOU MAY CALL (415) 252-4600. THIS LESSOR AND THIS NOTICE COMPLY WITH SAN FRANCISCO ADMINISTRATIVE CODE CHAPTER 37.9(a) SUBSECTION (1), ENACTED IN 1979, AMENDED THEREAFTER, IN THAT THE TENANTS HAVE FAILED TO PAY THE RENT TO WHICH THE LANDLORD IS LAWFULLY ENTITLED UNDER THE RENTAL AGREEMENT BETWEEN THE TENANTS AND THE LANDLORD.

_____   _____

DATE   SIGNATURE

Name, Title, and Address of Signatory

THREE DAY NOTICE TO PERFORM COVENANT

TO: _____and DOES I-X
       TENANT(S) IN POSSESSION

Please take notice that you have violated the following covenant(s) in your lease or rental agreement: *(State exact lease provision and the violation)*

_____

_____

YOU ARE HEREBY required within three (3) days to perform the aforesaid covenant(s) or to deliver up possession of the premises now held and occupied by you to *(landlord or landlord's agent)*_____,
who is located at *(address)*_____ and who is authorized to receive the same, being those premises situated in the City of _____, County of _____, State of California, commonly known as *(address)*_____.
If you fail to do so, legal proceedings will be instituted against you to reclaim said premises, to declare the forfeiture of the lease or rental agreement, and to recover such damages and attorney's fees as the law allows.

This notice is intended to be a three (3) day notice to perform the aforesaid covenant(s). If, after legal proceedings, said premises are recovered from you, the owner(s) will try to rent said premises for the best possible rent, giving you credit for sums received and holding you liable for any deficiencies arising during the term of said lease or rental agreement.

ADVICE REGARDING THIS NOTICE IS AVAILABLE FROM THE SAN FRANCISCO RENT STABILIZATION AND ARBITRATION BOARD. YOU MAY CALL (415) 252-4600. THIS LESSOR AND THIS NOTICE COMPLY WITH SAN FRANCISCO ADMINISTRATIVE CODE CHAPTER 37.9(a) SUBSECTION (2), ENACTED IN 1979, AMENDED THEREAFTER, IN THAT YOU HAVE VIOLATED A COVENANT OF YOUR TENANCY.

_____   _____
DATE   SIGNATURE

Name, Title, and Address of Signatory

THREE DAY NOTICE TO QUIT *(Nuisance)*

TO: _____and DOES I-X
            TENANT(S) IN POSSESSION

ADDRESS: _____

CITY OF   _____, CA _____

NOTICE IS HEREBY GIVEN that within three (3) days after service upon you of this Notice, you are required to quit and deliver up possession of the premises to *(landlord or landlord's agent)*_____, located at *(landlord's or agent's address)*_____ who is authorized to institute legal proceedings against you to recover possession of said premises and unlawful detainer damages.

You are being served with this Notice by reason of the fact that you have used the subject premises in a manner constituting a continuing nuisance, as defined by California Civil Code Section 3479, and pursuant to California Code of Civil Procedure, Section 1161(4), in that:

*(Date)*_____   *(Incident)*_____

_____

*(Further repeated or ongoing incidents)*_____

_____

ADVICE REGARDING THIS NOTICE IS AVAILABLE FROM THE SAN FRANCISCO RENT STABILIZATION AND ARBITRATION BOARD. YOU MAY CALL (415) 252-4600. THIS LESSOR AND THIS NOTICE COMPLY WITH SAN FRANCISCO ADMINISTRATIVE CODE CHAPTER 37.9(a) SUBSECTION (3), ENACTED IN 1979, AMENDED THEREAFTER, IN THAT THE TENANT IS COMMITTING OR PERMITTING TO EXIST A NUISANCE IN, OR IS CREATING A SUBSTANTIAL INTERFERENCE WITH, THE COMFORT, SAFETY, OR ENJOYMENT OF THE LANDLORD OR OTHER TENANTS IN THE BUILDING.

_____   _____
DATE   SIGNATURE

Name, Title, and Address of Signatory

THIRTY DAY NOTICE TO TERMINATE TENANCY

TO: _____and DOES I-X

TENANT(S) IN POSSESSION

PLEASE TAKE NOTICE THAT YOU ARE HEREBY required within thirty (30) days of the service upon you of this Notice to remove from and deliver up possession of the premises now held and occupied by you to *(landlord or landlord's agent)*_____, located at *(landlord's or agent's address)*_____ and who is authorized to receive the same, being those premises situated in the City of _____, County of _____, State of California, commonly known as *(address)*_____.

THIS NOTICE IS INTENDED for the purpose of terminating the month-to-month rental agreement by which you now hold possession of the above-described premises, and should you fail to comply, legal proceedings will be instituted against you to recover possession, to declare said rental agreement forfeited, and to recover DAMAGES for the period of the unlawful detention.

ADVICE REGARDING THIS NOTICE is available from the San Francisco Rent Stabilization and Arbitration Board. You may call (415) 252-4600.

THE RENT SHALL BE DUE AND PAYABLE to and including the date of termination of your tenancy.

THIS NOTICE IS BEING SERVED UPON YOU for the following reason(s) in accordance with the San Francisco Administrative Code Chapter 37.9(a) Subsection _____:

(Note: The reason for terminating tenancy must be in accordance with the local ordinance.)

_____

_____

_____   _____
DATE   SIGNATURE

Name, Title, and Address of Signatory

Glossary

breach of covenant: The breaking or nonperformance of a promise or term contained in a rental agreement.

capital improvement: Changes or additions to property which either materially add to its value, prolong its useful life, or adapt it to new uses; improvements beyond normal or delayed maintenance work.

case law: The body of controlling law as decided by Courts of Appeal.

contingency basis: A fee arrangement with an attorney who agrees to accept his fee only if there is a monetary outcome.

defendant: The person defending a lawsuit; the party against whom a complaint has been made in court.

demurrer: A legal attack upon the plaintiff's (e.g., landlord's) complaint in court which seeks to show that the complaint is somehow deficient; sometimes used to delay the proceedings in Unlawful Detainer cases.

deposition: The testimony of a witness outside of court, as a means of trial preparation; a word-for-word account is prepared which may be used in court.

duty to mitigate: The obligation of a landlord, if seeking to hold a tenant responsible to pay for the remaining lease term after vacating early, to lessen his or her losses by finding another tenant.

indemnify: To insure against or pay for loss or damage.

just cause: Recognized and approved reasons—e.g., nonpayment of rent, nuisance, owner move-in—allowing eviction of a tenant under a local rent control ordinance.

liability insurance: Insurance coverage for claims of others for injuries to themselves or their property.

Motion to Quash: A legal procedure by a defendant claiming the court should not hear the case because of a technical defect; usually results in a delay of several weeks.

Motion to Strike: A legal procedure used by a defendant to ask the court to eliminate part of the plaintiff's complaint; results in delaying an Unlawful Detainer case from proceeding to trial.

mutual release: An agreement by parties to a dispute by which each party gives up its claim against the other; typically prepared and signed when parties settle a lawsuit.

negligence: The failure to do something that a reasonable person would do; or the doing of something which a reasonable person would not do. The failure to take the appropriate care.

nuisance: Unreasonable, illegal, or disturbing use of property; interference with the enjoyment of neighbors; annoyance or disturbing of others.

ordinances: The laws of a city; state and federal laws are called statutes.

"personal service": The direct delivery of a notice or summons to a person by actually handing it to him or her.

plaintiff: The party who starts a lawsuit; the party who complains in a civil court action.

punitive damages: Financial compensation awarded by a court to a plaintiff beyond the amount the plaintiff has actually suffered. This award serves to punish the defendant.

"**quiet enjoyment**": The right of a tenant to enjoy possession of a rental unit in peace and without being disturbed.

rent control: The limitation imposed in certain cities on the amount of rent that can be charged to a residential tenant.

retaliatory eviction: The removal (or attempted removal) of a tenant when taken in reaction to the tenant exercising legitimate rights.

self-help: Taking action with legal consequences without obtaining judgment by a court.

statute: The law of a state, as passed by its legislature.

substantial rehabilitation/renovation: One of the recognized and allowable reasons under certain local ordinances allowing eviction of tenants so the landlord can do improvements or repairs to the property. Both the scope of the work required and whether the tenant can return after completion of it vary from city to city.

"**substituted service**": Proper but indirect delivery of a notice or summons; usually by posting on the premises, mailing, and/or delivery to someone else who is present.

Unlawful Detainer: The lawsuit used to remove a tenant from possession of property after the tenancy has been properly terminated.

vacancy control: A type of local rent control ordinance in which the rent cannot be raised to market value after a vacancy. The new tenant will have rent reduced by the local ordinance. (Being phased out state-wide.)

vacancy decontrol: A type of local rent control ordinance in which the rent can be raised to market value after a vacancy. The new tenant will have to pay market rent.

wrongful eviction: The illegal displacement of a tenant.

Index

Criminal prosecution: for assault, battery, and trespass, 59; civil penalties, 35; by District Attorney for wrongful evictions, 63; for illegal termination of a tenancy, 108; for landlord's use of "self-help" measures, 108; for violations of rent- and eviction- control laws, 35

"Curable breaches" of the rent law, 42, 109; lease violations, 42; nonpayment of rent, 42; Three Day Notice, 42, 109; Three Day Notice to Perform Covenant, 115

D

Damages: amount tripled by court in civil suits, 34, 155; civil suits to collect (e.g., excessive rent cases), 34; deducted from security deposit, 15, 125; destructive tenants, 57, 92, 94, 112; eviction for, 42, 55; in illegal eviction cases, 58, 62, 63; judgment in civil suits, 34; lawsuits to collect in Small Claims Court, 130; from vandalism, 93

Death, tenant's: disposition of personal property, 74; Probate Court order, 74; surviving spouse, 74

Default: in Unlawful Detainer cases, 123

Defective condition of rental property, 49

Defense techniques: owner's, 47; tenant's, in retaliation cases, 118

Delays in eviction actions, 110; cost of, 113; demurrer, 145. See also Chapter 25: Delaying Tactics

Demolition of rental property: a result of rent control, 40

Demurrer: tenant's use of as delaying tactic, 120; necessity for attorneys, 145

Discrimination/bias: age, 4; against families with children, 4, 10, 48; gender, 4, 47; marital status, 47; against minority groups, 6; national origin, 47; physical disability, 47; racial, 4; religious, 4; against rental applicants, 3–4, 47; against a tenant, 47, 145

Drug dealing, 92, 114

E

East Palo Alto, City of: "strict" rent control, 39, 41. See also Appendix A: Rent Control Ordinances

Economics: of rent control, 39; rent controls dysfunctional, 39–40. See also Chapter 8: Economic Impact

Emergencies: exits, 23; landlord access in, 22, 26, 27

Emotional distress claims: in illegal eviction cases, 58, 102; insurance coverage of, 18, 165; against landlords, 17, 19, 25, 133